The Pastoral Letters of George Fox
1643 – 1690

Charlotte Condia

Copyright 3rd Edition 2012 by Charlotte Condia

All rights reserved

No part of this book may be reproduced in any form, by photostat, microfilm, xerography, or any other means, or incorporated into information retrieval system, electronic or mechanical, without the written permission of the copyright owner.

Published by Sunrise Publication
3714 Hwy 28 #33
Las Cruces, NM 88005

This Book is dedicated, with many thanks, to Rebecca Richman without whose expert help I could never have finished it.

Preface

I see the life of George Fox, human founder of the Religious Society of Friends (Quakers), as a wonderful triumph of the human spirit over incredible adversity. Over the years I have come to admire him very much. The pastoral letters – there are 410 of them dating from 1650 to 1690 – are the best statements of his beliefs.

I am not an authority on George Fox. This book is an account of my experience of his ideas and beliefs through reading his letters. My interpretation of them is overly simplified and does not take into consideration the great depth of Fox's faith, his insights or the subtlety of his understanding. Pastoral letters are spiritual guidance to be read in public, most often to a Quaker Meeting. So, although Fox writes several pastoral letters on marriage, he does not mention his wife, Margaret Fell, because she is a private part of his life. I treated all the letters as a unit not being concerned if an idea is early or late or if it changes over Fox's lifetime. I have written about Fox's beliefs in the present tense for they live on today fresh and new in the letters. I rely mainly on the letters themselves, not using many other sources.

Canby Jones has done a very good service by making these letters so accessible and readable in his edition of them, *The Power of the Lord is over all, the Pastoral Letters of George Fox,* Friends United Press, Richmond, Indiana, Second Printing, 1990. This is where I read them. I also rely on Dr. Jones book, *George Fox's Attitude toward War.* Annapolis: Academic Fellowship, 1972, for Fox's position on violence.

I am indebted to my husband who answered such questions

as, "Is this George Fox or Scripture?" and "What does this passage from the Bible mean?" If I found a biblical passage difficult to understand, he would translate it from the Greek or Hebrew for me. He also translated from Italian the account of the release of two Quaker women held by the inquisition at Malta.

There are several ABC's for grownups to make difficult or unfamiliar information easier to understand and to show Fox's remarkable use of language. For the writer of alphabets, the letter X is a sound alike – excellent, exalted. Q is hard. When you have said "Quickener," there aren't many other choices. Z is also hard. Zest, zealous and zephyr. So I have just omitted Q and Z in some alphabets.

The alphabet on Christ tells a great deal about Fox's Christology. The language he uses is so beautiful and evocative that this ABC just wrote itself.

In Letter 64 written in 1654, Fox admonishes me to honor God with my words. This certainly is my intention; I hope that I have accomplished it.

Charlotte Condia
Las Cruces, New Mexico
Summer 2005

Contents

An ABC For Grownups To Introduce Quakers 1
No Man's Copy 5
Letter 56: To Call The Minds Out Of The Creatures Or How To Be A Mystic 10
George Fox's Time 15
The God Of The Quakers 20
Christ Has All Power 27
An ABC For Grownups Of Some Of The Names Of Christ Jesus 34
God Of Power 38
The Light 51
Creator, The Living God, Life, Father Of Life 63
God Of Unlimited Love 70
God Of Peace 74
The Quaker Peace Testimony 76
George Fox's Attitude Toward War 80
The Lamb 83
Spiritual Weapons 93
The Kingdom Of God And The Second Coming 96
The Quaker Path Of Holiness 101
Purity 108
The Behavior Of A Friend 114
Marriage In The Manner Of Friends 120
Friends Have Power 126
The Quaker Path Of Holiness 130

Meeting For Worship	133
The Business Meeting	135
Daughters Of Light	147
A Postscript	163
Sources	166

THE PASTORAL LETTERS OF GEORGE FOX

AN ABC FOR GROWNUPS TO INTRODUCE QUAKERS

ADVICES are principles for the spiritual guidance, caution and counsel of the Quaker Meeting.

Taking oaths implies a double standard of truth; AFFIRMING means that we must always tell the truth.

ANSWERING that of God in everyone is life's purpose for Quakers.

Spiritual BAPTISM is spiritual cleansing and it is the heart of the religious experience for Friends Water baptism is a public sign of what has happened inside; it is not necessary for Quakers. In BAPTISM of Suffering, we are made aware of the presence of the Holy Spirit through suffering. In this way our relationship with God is sealed.

Quakers read the BIBLE and try to understand and interpret it by their own experience in the Light and Presence of God

We COMMIT ourselves to a way of worship which allows God to teach and transform us.

CENTERING down is a way of concentrating on God and putting aside all other matters. Then we have CLEARNESS or clarity as to what God wants us to do with our lives.

The CLERK is the individual who directs the Meeting for Business.

A CONCERN is an urgent matter about which a person feels that God is calling him or her to pursue.

CONVINCED is accepting a new truth. An individual who becomes a Friend as an adult is a CONVINCED Friend.

DISCERNMENT is the wisdom to see the truth clearly.

DISOWNMENT is the practice of reading out of Meeting an individual Friend for such conduct as owning slaves or drinking too much alcohol.

Friends are the ELECT who dwell in the Light.

George FOX, G.F., is the human founder of the Religious Society of Friends

FRIENDS is the name we call ourselves. This name is based on John 15:14 in which Christ says "You are my Friends if you do what I command you."

What the world's people call Sunday; Quakers call FIRST day.

GOSPEL Order is about two things: the need to make provisions for those suffering and to set boundaries and standards for individual behavior.

George Fox opposed HAT HONOR, the removal of your hat to a "social superior." This is not just an empty act but one asserting equality and bearing witness to the HUMANITY of all people.

Friends are to maintain INTEGRITY, honesty and truthfulness, in all that we do and say. For we are in the life of the spirit.

All Friends are to take care to avoid all JARS and strife. For all jarrings are tares, out of the spirit. A JANGLER is an argumentative and quarrelsome person.

We are to KEEP our meetings in the Power of God.

The LIGHT Christ lives within us.

LEADINGS are direction from God on right ways to live.

Quakers should be examples and LET their LIVES speak.

MEETING for Worship is a group MYSTICAL experience in which we gather in silence to listen to God. It is held in a MEETING HOUSE. The MEETING for business is how God does His work in the world.

NOTIONS are beliefs which clutter the important truths of God and are out of harmony with them.

We have all ONE voice; we are written all in ONE another's hearts.

PEACEABLE Kingdom is the vision of all people living in harmony and neighborliness.

PLAIN Friends dress simply and use PLAIN language, thee and thou.

Friends are instructed in advices and QUERIES, or questions, which challenge and guide our faith and practice.

RIGHT order is doing things according to established Quaker practices; RIGHT order comes from the harmony of the Spirit within the Meeting.

The SENSE of the Meeting is more than consensus. It is a true unity, a sense of rightness of the point reached and a commitment to carry the decision forward. Consensus is a readiness to accept a decision reached by cooperative search.

A TESTIMONY is not just a verbal statement but also an action; the traditional TESTIMONIES are integrity, equality, community, simplicity and peace.

An UNPROGRAMMED Meeting has no pastor or formal program. Friends sit in silence waiting for God to fill their hearts and minds with love. Then they can share this love in VOCAL ministry.

WEIGHTY Friends, often elderly and with a great spirit, are to WALK cheerfully over the world, answering that of God in every one.

To EXERCISE is to explore an issue or concern.

In the beginning YEARLY meeting is a way of keeping track of Friends and giving some order to their lives when they suffer terrible persecution. YEARLY Meetings have always been for the comfort and joy of seeing one another. Today YEARLY MEETING still tries to give order and inspiration to Monthly Quaker Meetings so that Truth may prosper.

NO MAN'S COPY

Remarkable George Fox

William Penn, George Fox's contemporary, said of him that he is an original, no man's copy. He is one of a kind, an individual with exceptional natural capacity, natural ability, a God given gift, a creative person, who does original work. With a distinctive character and spirit, he influences others and the age in which he lives. He invents new religious ideas, looks at old ideas and makes them new and fresh or discovers new things in them. He recombines information in refreshing and different ways. The invention of new religious and social ideas is much more difficult than the invention of mechanical ones, and it happens less often.

The middle of the seventeenth century is a time of war, great differences between the rich and the poor. Religious systems, the courts and marriage law are in turmoil. Fox brings order to them for Friends. He is inspired so that he knows who God is and how God relates to people and people relate to God. With rare clarity he knows what is right and what is wrong and how to tell which is which. He knows how people should treat one another. How husbands should treat wives and vice versa; how parents should treat their children and businesspeople their customers. He makes new rules for the arranging of marriages.

With a consistent and orderly world view, Fox keeps the inward and outward life in harmony. Spiritual values permeate all his beliefs; every aspect of his life has a spiritual component. Stating that truth is the only way to communicate with others – by having only one standard – he simplifies the complex.

Fox understands people, sin, temptation, and addiction. Whatever any one is addicted to, the tempter comes in that thing. He uses it to take control of the individual. If the individual thinks that he or she will never overcome the temptation, help comes despite their expectations. The Light, the God within, shows the temptation. Fox makes withstanding temptation sound easy. "When it troubles you," he writes, "just sink down in that which is pure and all will be healed, hushed and fly away."

"Healed, hushed and fly away." What a wonderful phrase. Another, "prize the love of the Lord above all things."

Friends should keep out of the bustlings, of outward war. For those who are in the Lamb Christ are in the wise state and have spiritual weapons. To bustle is a verb; bustling is a gerund, a noun-verb. Fox adds an s and heightens the action and gives it more vitality. He does the same thing with require and requirings.

His language is poetic.

Yoke the oxen, bridle the horses, tame the wild heifers; bring them to Christ's yoke. Letter 65, 1654

Offer up the heavenly Fire in your Censers. For heavenly fire will consume all false offerings and sacrifice. Offer your heavenly fire, spiritual prayers, to Almighty God. Letter 36, 1653

A generous, good person, George Fox is filled with joy. Joy just seems to bubble up in him. He loves God but he also loves people. Genuinely good, generous people capable of loving others are rare. He piles up words that show this: goodness, peace, comfort, consolation, assurance, confidence and satisfaction, prosperity, praise, delight. He often uses the word tender: tender plants, tender Seed, tender sympathy.

Although he suffered many hardships, he is remarkably upbeat about life and often uses happy words like joy in his letters

> Heavenly joy fills your hearts.
> You are my joy and crown in the lord.
> Joy gladness and plenty.
> Joy be still.

Shine is another happy word.

> For they that turn many to Righteousness shall
> shine forever.
> The glorious Light is shining.
> The Light shines in the heart, in the face of Jesus Christ, and so we sees him in all our troubles and afflictions.
> Generation of the righteous will shine.

Often stern with Friends, he may holler at them, complain about them, call them every kind of sinner ever known; but he does like them. For he writes to them:

.

> Dear and tender Friends
> Dear Ones
> Dear Hearts and Babes of Christ
> My Dearest Hearts
> Dear Friends everywhere
> Dearly Beloved Friends

He ends some letters with the phrase, "so no more but my love to you all."

He blesses Friends:

> So the God of Life be with thee!
> God Almighty bless you and prosper his work.
> May you live in light, love, and life.

He makes whole what others only see in part, a complete plan for how to live a holy life. He gives the answers to such questions as:
Who is God?
What is our relationship with God? What is His relationship to us?
How are we to live in the world?
How do we behave toward others, to ourselves?
What are our responsibilities to others and to ourselves?
What is moral and good and what is not?
How do we live a peaceful life?

Fox believes that Friends should live in the world with a simple lifestyle, be in the world but not consumed by it. Friends are to have productive, meaningful lives loving and serving God. If they are persecuted and have their means of livelihood stolen, they are to stand up to their persecutors.

Eternity is not an excuse for oppressing people here and telling them that they will get their reward later. Fox also appreciates that even the simplest lifestyle requires resources. So he organizes Friends for defense against persecution to protect themselves. If they are imprisoned or have their lands confiscated, he shows them the most effective way to confront their persecutors in a non-violent way.

A man of peace, Fox could not condone war in any form or participate in it for any reason. He did not resist violent attacks upon himself but accepts suffering even though he believes that those who persecute and kill are traitors to Christ. He prays for and blesses his persecutors. For if you love your enemy, you cannot kill them.

Confident that God specially chose and shaped him, Fox believes that he is called to be a saint and live a life of purity, holiness and innocence. His job is to love and worship God, live a life of generosity and peace, treat other persons with respect and courtesy and try to do some good in the world. He also believes that he has authority by the Power of God to judge, if he judges with the Spirit of Truth and by the Light; he also has the authority to understand the powers of darkness and to trample upon this power and its authority. A moralist, a social revolutionary, an egalitarian, a preacher and teacher but ultimately he is a mystic and in Letter 56 written in 1653, he tells Friends how they can be mystics, too.

LETTER 56: TO CALL THE MINDS OUT OF THE CREATURES OR HOW TO BE A MYSTIC

A Blessing: God Almighty bless, guide and keep you all in his Wisdom.

Fox, the mystic, writes of how he understands and knows God. The greeting – to all Friends of the Lord everywhere – shows he believes that everyone can be a mystic and know God. (Christ in the male and female also shows this.) All we have to do is pay attention to the Light within us. And He will renew every ones minds and turn them inward to find God and worship Him. We should turn our minds away from "creatures," the created world. Fox wants us to get our minds off all externals and concentrate on worshiping the Living God, Christ, the Light and the Seed within and try to acquire things above. A pure mind is one that focuses inward towards God, without any distractions of earthly things. (A "virgin mind" is a pure innocent mind turned toward God.) We are to know our pure minds which deal with things that are true and actually exist in each of us.

When Fox uses the name Babes for Friends it means innocence and purity. The Babe is born again. This is the Quaker version of being born again. The pure Babe, the Friend, is born in the virgin mind, the pure innocent mind, turned inward to God. The Babes food--Christ, the Light—nourishes up to eternal life. In Letter 15, 1652 Fox expresses this idea of being born again in a slightly different way: "Friends, Babes in Christ, are born again of the immortal Seed and bow down to nothing but the Lord God."

These babes, children are presented with heavenly Wisdom from above, from the pure, living God, and not from the devil who is of the earth. If we hate the Light, it means our minds are turned outward to the world, not inward to God. Friends with the old nature – before we turned inward to God – hear but with an evil mind. We can't understand for we are concentrating on the things of the world, not on the heavenly message. This keeps us from seeing God clearly. The reward for those who serve the pure God night and day is to enjoy Peace which has no end.

Fox gives us a hard thing to do then shows how it can be done. He knows that the Lord God Almighty will be with us and will renew and regenerate our creative minds and keep us turned to Himself to worship and serve him.

Benediction: The Lord God Almighty be with you all and keep you turned to God to worship the Creator and serve him, not the creature.

God Is One

Based on his experience as a mystic, Fox believes that God lives within us. He knows and communicates with this God within. Friends are able to know and communicate with God also. One of Fox's greatest contributions to religious knowledge is that it is possible to know God.

Everyone can know God:

> know the things of God for His Truth does flourish.
> know the Spirit of God which He pours on all flesh.
> know his Son, Jesus Christ, who is eternal Life
> know the Power of Christ for He has all power in heaven and earth.
> know Christ, the second Adam, who enlightens.
> know Christ, the way to God.
> know the scriptures through the Light.

Friends, familiar with the first two—that it is possible to know and communicate with God--just take them for granted, not thinking how remarkable they are. The third—God is One—is less familiar but equally remarkable. Fox's most insightful mystical experience may be the awareness that God is One. He addresses God with many names—Light, Lord of hosts, Pure, Living God Eternal, Exalted, Lord God Almighty, Creator, Power, Wisdom—but God is One. (This is not a list of the attributes of God; these are God.) Fox admonishes us to dwell in the Power of the Lord, in the Seed of God, for this will keep us clear in our understanding. God, the Seed, the Light will reign in us and we will reign over the world. The Seed of God will reign in us all who is but One in all. God is One, the Word is One, the Light is One, and the Spirit is One.

In Letter 4 he writes, "Mind the Light, that all may be refreshed one in another and all in One." There are not individual Lights; the Light is one. The Light is consistent, doesn't differ in different persons, male or female, young or old. Always the same, it doesn't differ throughout time. Fox gives God, Christ and the Light many names. But there is a consistency, harmony, unity to them. For him, God is one experience with a great deal of variety.

God is One.
Son of God is One
Christ is One.
One Christ who calls all to repentance.
One Head who calls the repentant up to Himself.
Light of God is but One.
One Light who leads you out of darkness into the everlasting Day.
One Eye which is the Light.
Lord of hosts
Pure
Living God
Eternal
Exalted
Lord God Almighty
Creator
Wisdom.
Power of the Lord
Peace
one Father
Word is One.
Life is One,
Eternal Spirit is One.
One spirit which baptizes all into one body where there is pureness and oneness.
Because the Seed Christ is One, all who are in the Spirit are One.
Seed of God is One.
Seed Christ is One, so all who are in the
Spirit are One
Power is One.
One Power that raises up the Seed.
One fire which consumes all that the Light discovers to be evil.

Trinity

So all walk in it the Light to receive the Son, in which Light is the unity which brings fellowship with the father and Son.
Letter 25 1653

Fox uses the names of the Persons of the Trinity: God, Jesus, Holy Spirit, Crucified God, Sun of Righteousness, Holy Ghost, and Father. He is not a Trinitarian, but believes that God is One. The term trinity doesn't appear in the pastoral letters; it doesn't appear in the Bible. Fox would have been familiar with the term as it had been around since the beginning of the third century AD when Origen in the East and Tertullian in the West first used it at about the same time. As it is not in the Bible, this may be the reason that he did not use it. On the other hand, he may not have used it because it is not part of his experience. As we have noted above he sees God as One.

George Fox's Time

Cuius *regio, eius religio*. The religion of the ruler is the religion of the country. This is the principle agreed upon at the Peace of Westphalia, which, in 1648, ended the Thirty Years War – fought principally in central Europe – between the Catholic and the Lutheran forces. "Liberty of conscience" as such is not a well understood concept anywhere. If a person wouldn't practice the religion of their ruler, he or she was free, in theory, to emigrate. Property is left behind, though.

This is the situation in England. Everyone and everything is subject to the King and magistrates – preacher, prophet, apostle. There is only one religion in the state, and the state decides what this religion will be. Religious beliefs and religious services, readymade, must be accepted because they are ordained by Crown, parliament and Privy Counsel. A rigid class structure existed with little personal freedom and little, if any, consulting of one's own private judgment.

This is the England – marked by war, social stratification, and poverty – into which Fox is born in 1624. Religious systems, the courts and marriage law are in turmoil, and Fox brings some order to them for Friends. He also brings order to the Religious Society of Friends through the Meeting for Worship and the Meeting for Business in which God's work in the world is done.

When he dies in London in 1691, there are probably 50,000 Friends in England. He has created a local and regional structure which allows the headquarters in London to keep in touch with events and developments in even the smallest communities. Lines of authority and mutual concern are clear. Beginning in 1682 the London Yearly Meeting knows the condition of local communities, how many friends are in prison, and organizes all Friends into Meetings for Suffering for defense against persecution.

> ***For we here are under great persecution, between thirteen and fourteen hundred in prison: an account of which has lately been delivered to the King. Besides the great spoil and havoc which is made of Friends; goods by informers; and besides the great spoil upon two-thirds of our estates, and upon the twenty pound a month acts, and for not going to the steeple house; and besides many are imprisoned and premunired for not swearing allegiance, both men, women, widows and maids; and many are fined and cast into prison, as rioters, for meeting to worship God; and we are kept out of our Meetings in streets and highways in many places of the land, and beaten and abused; therefore prize the Liberty, both natural and spiritual, that you enjoy.*** Letter 386, 1683

Non-conformists religious groups, such as Baptists, refuse to comply. These dissenting congregations are made up of individuals who pride themselves on their independence. For them, human reason and common sense have their place beside the Bible and church authority. Chapel and ministers belong to the congregation, not to the squire and his lady. These non-conformists influence Fox.

In my opinion, though, the most important influence for good on Fox is that both the Bible and pamphlets, which are small booklets containing arguments on a particular religious subject, are in English, as are religious services. (The mass is no longer said in Latin, and Anglican services are in English.) So Fox is familiar with the Bible, pamphlets on religious subjects, and services in English.

The first Church of England prayer book is issued in English in 1549. The Bible has been translated earlier into Anglo-Saxon. In the fourteenth century, John Wycliffe translates it into English, and recruits traveling preachers to spread its use. In 1525 William Tyndale translates most of the Bible from the original Greek and Hebrew. A second edition of this translation comes out in 1525. "I had perceived by experience," said Tyndale "how that it was impossible to establish the lay people in any truth, except the scripture were plainly laid before their eyes in their mother tongue."

The Geneva Bible. first published in 1557, is based on the best texts and scholarship available at the time. King James I authorized the translation which we know today as the King James Bible in 1611. No attempt is made to force it on the Church of England; it becomes popular on its own merit. The Geneva Bible is still regarded with favor. George Fox knowsboth well and he is deeply influenced by them. His writings are filled with direct quotes and allusions to them. He believes that the Light inspires the Bible, or as he calls them Scriptures, and helps us understand them. But the Bible is only a declaration of the fountain, not the fountain itself. Fox gives a long and elaborate biblical argument for a certain idea. Then he says something to the effect that Christ is the answer; He is sufficient.

Although it is a crime to repudiate England's state run church, on a more day to day basis Friends annoy poor married Anglicans clergy with large families with the Quaker belief that paid ministers are not true messengers of Christ.

The restoration of Charles II in 1660 is only a change of persecutors for Friends. The Quaker Act becomes law in May 1662. Hounded for refusing to swear the oath of allegiance to the king, for refusing to pay tithes, it is unlawful for Friends *not to go to* Anglican services. It is unlawful for them *to go to* Quaker Meetings. No more than four Quakers can meet at any one time for any purpose. Fines, imprisonment and finally transportation to a penal colony are the penalties. (Fortunately transportation is such a hard thing to arrange that few Friends suffered this penalty.) By 1672 more than 6000 Friends have served prison terms under King Charles. Four hundred and fifty of them die in prison and another fifty die shortly after their release because of the terrible conditions there.

An ancient fourteenth century law of Praemunire—Fox spells it premunire—is revived to deal with those who refuse the oath of allegiance to the King. Under this law, Friends' property is confiscated, their civil rights lost and they are put into prison with the length of imprisonment "at the king's pleasure" or for terms that could last indefinitely. This provision of the law accounts for the fact that many Friends are confined for such long terms. George Fox's longest imprisonment—from First month 1664 to Ninth month 1666—is due to this.

Activities central to being a Quaker are criminalized. Charges include vagrancy, blasphemy and the refusal to pay tithes or swear oaths. Informing on Quakers became a way to make money for some religious and civil authorities.

Charles II may have been looking for possessions and land to fill the royal coffers or scapegoats because 7000 had died of the plague in 1665 in London. Friends are persecuted and beaten. Meetings for Worship are broken up and Meeting houses destroyed. Fox helps early Friends cope in both a spiritual and a practical way. In his estimation, early Friends suffer the most of any people in England.

George Fox sees life with rare clarity. He loves and knows God and expresses his love and knowledge through his wonderful ability with words. He is able to make fine distinctions and sees the nature of God as the Light, Christ's nature as the Light, and that the Light lives within everyone. His experience and understanding of the Bible – which he knowsbackwards and forwards and inside out – is immense.

Fox understands, more clearly than most, the difference between right and wrong.

Although his social position places severe limitation on his life, Fox sees genuine equality for everyone rather than individuals confined to strict classes. He also sees that these individuals have a right to liberty of conscience. Imprisoned, beaten, denied the right to worship as he chose, he still is able to see that disputes can be settled by peaceful means, and that war and violence are not justified.

More than a very bright, capable person, Fox has a passion for life and leaves a legacy for the future.

THE GOD OF THE QUAKERS

An ABC For Grownups Of Some Of God's Names

Almighty All-Sufficient Beginning Beautiful Bountiful Beloved Creator Dread Eternal Everlasting Father Friend Faithful Forgiving Good Glorious Generous Governor Gracious Hallowed Heavenly Holy Immortal Invisible Judge King Lord Living Light Love Life Mercy Near Omnipotent Order Peace Power Quaker Rest Righteous Safety Shepherd Truth Trust Universal Unity Unchangeable Wisdom Yes

God's Name

In some religious systems there is power in knowing God's name. An individual with this kind of knowledge has dominance over God. Somewhat like a phone solicitor who has your name and acts as if he is entitled to pester you. Fox names God, Christ, the Light many names but he is not a pal with God; he would never wear a T-shirt claiming to love Jesus. His attitude is one of great reverence and awe. God's name is not an instrument of magic or a threat, but a gift of revelation. God's name is not a secret, making an intermediary necessary but can be known to everyone. Why does George call God so many different names? These names are not just a list of the attributes of God. He overflows with such a passionate love of God that one name is just not sufficient to express this love.

Glory and praise be to his Name forever.

The crown of Fox's experience is his knowledge and passionate love of God and his ability to communicate this to others. He shows that it is possible to know and love God. He writes about this love and his deep belief in Him in an extraordinary way that few people have. An expert in knowing and loving God, he doesn't compartmentalize, put God in a corner of his life. His love of God fills his whole life. There is a goodness, wholesomeness, depth and genuine excitement to this belief that isn't often found in this world.

Fox believes in a Living God who is to be praised and worshiped; God has terrible power but still cares for all people. When he writes about God, Fox writes about something that he knows very well. For him, God is a God at hand, an immediate God, a God who deals with him directly – right now, right here, an intimate, personal God.

God is real, genuine. It is possible to know Him. However, if Fox is to know God, he must not just live a good life but a life of extraordinary goodness, must spend a good bit of his time getting to know God. (Well, really, he spends all his time doing this.) Then God shows him what he wants him to do with his life. This is all worthwhile because the prize at the end is great.

God deals directly with Fox without an intermediary, just the individual and God; so, he can be close to God, speak to Him. This closeness is costly, though. The commitment and dedication, the moral life, the single-mindedness that Fox needs to obtain this prize are tremendous. "Let not the mind go forth from God! For if it do, it will be stained, venomed and corrupted."

This getting to know God must be done in fear, reverence and awe. But Fox makes it sound easy. He turns his mind within and waits until an entrance is made into his soul. It is not only possible to get to know God, but it is everyone's job in life.

Fox believes that it is possible to know God, the things of God. the Life that stands in God, know Him by whom the world was made. All with the Spirit of God might know God, His Son, Jesus Christ.

It is possible to know the Power of the mighty God, Christ, and the Light. All may know what it is to follow the Lamb, know the Seed of God in one another, and know the Life and Power of God in ourselves. Fox knows God as a God who loves the righteous; One who punishes the disobedient.

It is possible, not only for Fox, but for Friends, to know and feel God, Christ, the Seed of God.

> ***Dear Friends and brethren, feel the Seed of God in yourselves, who is the heir of the Power of God, that you may inherit the promise of the Gospel.***

He spells out some of his beliefs about God in the letter to the governor of Barbados. God is:
>Power, almighty, omnipotent
>only wise
>immortal, everlasting
>invisible
>a living God, creator of all things, both in heaven and earth
>preserver of all that he hath made
>God over all
>God of heaven

Power is the name that George Fox uses most often for God. He has incredible power but still cares for all people. Fox knows the Bible – the King James and the Geneva – backwards and forwards and inside out. His knowledge and experience of it are immense. He quotes from it and alludes to it often in his letters. The Bible gives him much of his language about God and his experience showed him what to do with this language. His perception of the Power of God came from both sources. He takes this information and gives it new content and energy. He uses the word power both as a name for God and as a divine attribute. Christ has all power; Friends also have power. God confers inner strength and purity on His saints, His elect, His Friends. Power protects them from those in the world who would harm them; He defends them from the devil, the power of darkness.

Power as a Name of God

Fox uses Power as a name for God. In Letter 206, 1661 he writes:

Know and feel the Power and the Seed.
Partake of the Power.
Shod in the Power.

In Letter 104, 1655:

Hasty spirits which will run without the Power.
There is safety in the Power.
The Power being lived in, it keeps you over the world in the dread and majesty of   Truth.
the Power keeps you over the world in cleanness and newness of life.
All spirits that are unruly and out of the Power.

That which lives in the Power is begotten by the Seed Christ.
In your meetings know and feel the Power.

Fox also uses "the Word" six times as a name for Christ in the letter 104. The name Word is Biblical and the usage is not in question. As the format the Power and the Word are the same, it seems reasonable to think that Fox intends Power as a name for God.

Lord God Almighty as a Name for God

Fox uses Almighty, which means powerful, as a name for God.

> God Almighty increase and multiply us...
> Keep our minds in the strength of the Almighty.
> May The Lord God Almighty preserve us.
> So God Almighty be among you to do his will in his Love.
> So God Almighty be with you all!
> The Almighty is a God of Love.
> The Almighty supports us.
> The God Almighty guides and prospers us.
> The God Almighty is Power and Truth.
> The Lord God Almighty keeps you turned to the Creator.
> The Lord God Almighty has discovered you.

Almighty is also an attribute of God; God is all-sufficient and Almighty.

The Mighty God Of Power

Fox uses mighty as an attribute of God, not a name. Friends should know the Power of the mighty God. His arm, how it works; the hand how it carries them. This mighty Power of God enables them to stand over all the world. It also enables Friends to trample, tread and bend the beast's and dragon's worship and false prophets before the mighty God.

Omnipotent, which means all powerful, is a word that can only apply to God. But this all powerful God hears the cries of the oppressed and afflicted ones, day and night. Only wise would seem to mean that only God has perfect knowledge and wisdom, and that all other knowledge and wisdom are less than this.

The most powerful human that Fox knows is the King of England. Although he preaches to or at him, sends him petitions, tells him what he is doing wrong, he is well aware of his great earthly power. However God is the King of kings and Lord of lords, the strong, all-sufficient, omnipotent God. He has all power but still sees all the actions of men. Friends should be loyal to this King who conquered the devil, death and hell.

Power Of The Father

Fox also calls the Father both Power and powerful. Christ, who knew no sin, was crucified for us in the flesh, buried, rose again the third day by the power of His Father. This powerful Father and eternal God is due all glory, honor and thanks forever.

Power Of The Lord God

Often bruised, bloodied and sore but by the power of the Lord, Fox is refreshed. Friends are to keep their minds in the strength of the Almighty, not in weakness, nor in infirmities but in the Lord's Power for It will bring all their persecutors to rags and poverty. They should know the Power of the Lord God. and heed nothing but His Life and power. (According to Fox, God loves Friends more than others. He will protect them. In this instance reducing their persecutors to poverty.)

The Lord's Power could move Friends to preach the Gospel and sound deep to the Witness of God in every man.

CHRIST HAS ALL POWER

The Letter To The Governor Of Barbados

Because of the "many scandalous lies and slanders that have been cast upon Friends, saying that we deny Christ Jesus," Fox writes, in 1671, a letter to the Governor of Barbados defending them. "All of our books and declarations clearly testify to the contrary." When Friends talk about this letter today, they will say that it is the "closest thing that Quakers have to a creed" or that it is "sort of a creed." But the letter is the Nicene and Apostle's creed in Fox's own language. The language is scriptural but the creeds influence what he says.

We own and believe in
> Jesus the beloved and begotten Son of God, who was conceived by the Holy Ghost and born of the Virgin Mary, and who is the express image of the invisible God by whom all things were created.
>
> He, who knew no sin, was crucified for us in the flesh, buried, rose again the third day by the power of His Father.
>
> He ascended up into heaven and now sitteth on the right hand of God.
>
> He is our wisdom and righteousness, our prophet.
>
> He is the Quickening Spirit, the second Adam, the Lord from heaven.

He brings the oaths of God, the new covenant of light, life, grace and peace.

He alone is our Redeemer and Savior.

An orthodox Christian, Fox believes that Christ is God's Son, the way to God, the Second Adam, who never fell, eternal life. He is the Light who has enlightened every man who has come into the world – Turks, Jews, Moors, Christians. He is the Life, the Word, who brings the glad tidings of salvation. Christ is the Mediator who makes peace; the Life that was with the Father before the world began. He is all virtue.

Christ bore the sins and iniquities of all mankind, and was an offering for the sins of the whole world so we may have Life through Him. Christ did not die as he was God, but as he was man. He suffered in the flesh, died and was crucified as he was man, not as he was God. For the Eternal God was not crucified and died. For Christ, the man, said as he hung on the cross, "My God, my God, why hast thou forsaken me?"

Fox's phrase, "as he was man," is entirely orthodox. He means that it is the human nature of Christ, not the divine nature, which was crucified and rose. There is no suggestion that Christ is God at some times, but not at others.

Christ Has All Power

Christ is the answer for Fox. Through His power and strength, Friends will be able to do all things. Power is Christ's name: the Name of Christ who is Power and Light in you all. Christ has all Power in heaven and earth given to Him, that all may feel his living and divine Presence among them.

King of Kings and Lord of lords, He has ascended above all principalities, powers and thrones. This powerful, all sufficient God is also the true shepherd who protects the lambs from dogs and feeds them in green pastures. This shepherd gives life abundantly.

And there is the safe sitting in Christ, the new and living Way, the Word of God, the Power of God, the Light, the Life and Truth, the first, the last, the beginning, the ending, in whom is no shadow of turnings nor variableness. The saints sit in Christ, the head, and there are the exceeding riches and the kindness known again. Letter 222, section 8, 1662

The Cross of Christ is the Power of God. Friends should bow to it – the real Cross – not a stick, stone or piece of wood. Power and Spirit meet together in Jesus Christ, the Lord's Light who has all Power in heaven and earth given to him.

Jesus Christ is sovereign Lord of the Universe. He has power over all men so they owe Him allegiance. The conviction that Christ rules in power as universal king is central to Fox's faith.

Fox gives Christ many wonderful names. These names are not just attributes but indications of Fox's experience of Christ and of his love for Him. For Fox, Christ is always the answer, there is no other way to God but by Christ Jesus. He and understands Christ in a remarkable way as the Light, the Seed, the Second Adam and the Lamb.

Christ is the Power of God, the new and living Way, the Word of God.

The Cross of Christ is the Power of God. Friends should bow to it – the real Cross, not a stick, stone or piece of wood.

Power and Spirit meet together in Jesus Christ, the Lord's Light. He is the sovereign Lord of the Universe; He has power over all men so they owe Him allegiance. The conviction that Christ rules in power as universal king is central to Fox's faith.

Seed and Power

Fox uses the name Seed for Christ. The name is Biblical: Now to Abraham and his seed were the promises made. He saith not, And to seeds, as of many; but as of one, And to the seed, which is Christ. Galatians 3:16. But he takes the biblical terminology and develops it in new directions. For the Seed is Power but He also lives in Power. This Seed Power, which keeps Friends over the world in cleanness and newness of life, is begotten by Him. Christ the Seed also breaks the serpent's power and crushes him to pieces.

Friends also are the royal Seed of God who are to meet in the Seed in the Power of God which was before enmity was. They are to feel the Seed who is the heir of the Power of God.

Fox had been premunired because he could not take an oath. But the Lord's Seed and Power is over all so he is able to endure.

The Lamb and Power

Fox advises Friends to dwell in patience and love of God and one another. The Lamb must have the victory over them all, the wild beasts in the field who are in the fall from God. And though the beast's horns be ever so long. Fox seems to give the Lamb Christ an extra bit of Power for the Lamb will conquer and take away the sin. He makes war in righteousness and will rule, subdue, conquer and be victorious over human sin and the power of the devil. Fox doesn't think it a mystery that the Lamb should have victory over all the wild, uncontrollable, the wolfish part of human nature, for He is clean and holy.

The Lamb defends Friends under persecution. So all thanks be to Him, who is come to rule alone in his saints. The righteous should rejoice for the Lamb is victorious over the beast that pushed at Him.

Friends have both the Power of God and the Power of the Lamb Christ to defend and help them. So they should not fear suffering for Christ suffered. They should let their backs and cheeks be ready to the "smiters." They should not fear him that can kill the body only, but can't hurt the soul. In this way they will be preserved in gentleness and in boldness by the Lord God Almighty.

Friends should be faithful to Christ the Lamb, who is their crown. The Lamb was slain from the foundation of the world but reigns over all principalities and powers. (Principalities and powers are angelic beings, often evil ones.) The Lamb takes away human sin and breaks the devil's power over it. He will be victorious so Friends should follow Him.

In the day of the Lamb's Power the church in her glory will appear and Friends are the gold tried in the fire. They have been tried by goods spoiling, by bonds, by whippings, by "mockings" and reproach. Some have been tried unto the death and have proved to be pure gold that has come forth brighter and brighter.

Fox has great concern for Friends so he writes with great tenderness to them in Letter 192, 1660 "From a lover of your soul's eternal Good, and of your establishment in Righteousness and Peace in this day of the Lamb's Power, Glory to the Highest forever!"

Second Adam

One of the many names Fox gives Christ is the Second Adam who is Power, who must rule in people's hearts in obedience. As He does in all that have Power and enjoy Life. (Fox is always surprising you. Who would have expected enjoy Life in this context.)

Married To Power?

Fox uses marriage in a symbolic way and writes that Friends should be married and joined to the royal Seed, Christ and the Lamb. Christ has Truth and Power, so we should keep marriage with Him our first love, the holy one, the Just one, the Light, the Truth and Power of God, who makes an end to all unholiness.

Keep your Faith in the Power of God, which will bring you to the Marriage of the Lamb, by which Power you may have oil in your lamps that your lamps may burn always.

> Prisons, fetters, dungeons and sufferings what are they to you who are married to the Lamb, who was slain from the foundation of the world, against whom they warred and banded themselves who breaks their bonds asunder, whom neither death, grave, nor all the powers were able to hold nor contain, but overall he rose and

reigns, till he has made his enemies his footstool." (Letter 206, 1661)

A Blessing: Dear Friends, my love to you all in the Seed of Life and Peace which flow as a river. Letter 354, 1679

AN ABC FOR GROWNUPS OF SOME OF THE NAMES OF CHRIST JESUS

Amen, Anchor Author Baptizer, Bishop Bridegroom Comforter Counselor, Covenant, Cross, Crown, Day Star, Emmanuel, Foundation First and Last, Governor, Green Tree, Guide, Head, Holy, Heavenly Instructor, Heavenly and Spiritual man, Holy Pattern, Head Hope of Glory, Husband, Inward, Judge, Justice, Judgment, Joy, King, Lamb, Leader Life Light, Living Stone, Lord Mediator Mountain New Covenant One Head Orderer, Overseer, Peace, Prophet, Priest, Quickening Spirit Ransom Redeemer Refreshment, Redeemer, Reconciler, Ransom, Reason Reconciler Redeemer, Resurrection, Resurrection Rest Revelation Righteous Rock of Ages Root Rose Ruler Sanctuary, Savior, Second Adam, Seed, Shepherd, Sun of Righteousness, Shield and Buckler, Sign and wonder, Son of God, Stone, Sufferer Teacher Topstone Tree Truth, Unchangeable Unity, Universal, Vine Victory Wings Way Wisdom Word Example Yoke Zeal

* * * * * * * * * * *

Believe in Jesus Christ, the Light and walk by that Faith which he is the AUTHOR of.

May you all be settled in Christ Jesus who was dead but is ALIVE again.

Everyone get oil in their lamps that they may arise at the hearing of the heavenly Voice of the BRIDEGROOM and enter with him.

And so in him be faithful, who is our CROWN. Let no man take our CROWN from us.

You have a Light which you do well to take heed unto that shines in a dark place, until the Day dawn and the DAY STAR arise in our hearts.

EVERLASTING COMMANDER who says love your enemies.

Christ, the Amen, the FIRST and the LAST, the Top and Cornerstone. In him sit down in Life, Peace and Rest.

Christ is the GREEN TREE which never withers.

Christ, the HEAVENLY and Spiritual man, by whom the world was made.

None become sons of God, but by receiving Christ, the HOPE OF GLORY, the purifier.

The Light Christ, the ILLUMINATOR.

Christ sets up an INWARD, spiritual ministry, a spiritual worship and Fellowship, a Church without spot or wrinkle and a religion that is pure from above

Every one of you, hear his voice that speaks from heaven, whose voice shakes the earth and the heavens also and this must be shaken and removed, both the heavens and the earth, before that appears that can never be shaken, the noble, royal Seed, elect and precious, before the world began. In him you shall know that which cannot be shaken. There is the true JOY.

Christ is KING over all the earth and has all Power in heaven and earth. He is KING of KINGS and Lord of Lords. Let Him reign in all your hearts by Faith.

Dwell in the LIGHT of Christ. Bring all to believe in the LIGHT, to give them the knowledge of the Glory of God in the face of Jesus Christ from whom the LIGHT comes

Christ, who was before death, is the pasture of LIFE.

Christ is the deliverer and MEDIATOR and the intercessor, that makes Peace between everyone and God.

MOUNTAIN Christ fills the whole earth.

Keep your meetings gathered into the NAME of Christ Jesus who is Prince of Life and Peace.

And so, all strive to be of one mind, heart, soul, Spirit and Faith, living together in Unity, having ONE HEAD.

Christ ORDERS with his Light and Life in the hearts of all believers.

God's Son, a PROPHET to open to you; a PRIEST to sanctify you; an everlasting PREACHER whom God has anointed to preach. Christ, the PROMISE, who opens and none can shut.

QUICKENING Spirit who destroys death and the power of it.

The ROCK, the Lord from heaven, RESURRECTION and Life.

In him, the SECOND ADAM, you will not be weary, nor faint, nor think the time long of our sufferings. In Him you will have Power and enjoy Life.

Christ is the TREE, that stands in the midst of God's Garden, whose leaf never fades, nor fruit fails. But the fruit feeds all the living and the leaves heal the nations.

Dwelling all in Christ Jesus who is UNCHANGEABLE, we come to judge all the changeable ways and worship.

VICTORY through Christ the true VINE.

Keep under the WINGS of Christ who destroys the destroyers.

Know the true WORD so that you may be sanctified and reconciled to God.

Take Christ as your eXample that there be no strife among you; take Christ as your eXample and cry, "Father forgive them." Exalt Him in your assemblies.

Collar the oxen, bridle the horses, tame the wild heifer. Bring them to Christ's YOKE so that they may see their way of salvation.

Clothed with the ZEAL of Christ, stand against all that is contrary to the Light.

GOD OF POWER

An ABC For Grownups Of The Characteristics Of The Universal God Of Power

---

Power ABOLISHES Death

It was in the BEGINNING.

All be kept and preserved by His holy Power so that you may be the CAMP of God. (Letter 412, 1687)

Power DISCOVERED us.

Is EVERLASTING   FELLOWSHIP, GLORIOUS

Power is HABITATION.

It will   INCREASE all the Lord's people everywhere.

Power is the promise of   JOY.

KNOW the Lord God of Power and feel the banner of LOVE and MERCY.

Is NEWNESS of life.

> POWER IS ORDER; It is OVER ALL
> Power PRESERVES
>
> REFRESHES, RENEWS, SUPPLIES all things needful. (Letter 398, 1684
>
> The Almighty SUPPORTS us; there is SAFETY in His Power. SHOD in the Power.
>
> Power and TRUTH make an end to all UNHOLINESS.
>
> Be VALIANT in the Power of God, VALIANT for His Truth.
>
> Power guides us in all His WISDOM.

Some Characteristics Of God's Power

Power Preserves

The Power of God and the Lord God Almighty is incredible. It was in the beginning before the Fall, before the power of darkness. It will preserve and increase all the Lord's people everywhere. God wishes Friends well; Fox wishes Friends well, too. "I desire that the Lord may grant that you may all be kept and preserved by His holy Power, on His holy Mountain, that you may be the Camp of God." (412)

In his testimony of how the Lord sent him forth at first in the year 1643 Fox anthropomorphized God and writes of how the Lord's arm and Power preserve and support him. He does the same thing in Letter 398.

Dear Friends whom the Lord does support, and has supported by his eternal Arm and Power to stand for his Glory. God is all-sufficient and Almighty to support you all, and to supply you with all things needful.

God's Power Is a Blessing

The Lord God Almighty keep you in His Power for it preserves and nourishes living babes with Food from the God of Life.

God Almighty preserve you that you may spread his blessed Truth abroad, and answer it in all people Amen.

Power Is Also a Benediction

The Lord God of Power be with you all, my dear hearts so that you may all be ordered to his glory. So that you may feel the banner of Love over you. Fare you well. (104)

Truth and Wisdom

The God Almighty is Power and blessed Truth. It is possible to obtain the promise of this power of Truth through the Word in the heart. Then this blessed Truth should be spread abroad for Truth and Power make an end to all unholiness.

Power is Truth so answer the Spirit of God in all people.

Everyone should be valiant in the Power of God, valiant for His Truth. Then they may live and reign doing the Truth to all by which all may see over that which burdens the creation.

Power blesses, guides, and keeps us in all His Wisdom. So Friends should be faithful in his Power through which they may discern Wisdom and have clear and pure understanding in the Power

Power Discovered Us

The Lord God Almighty has discovered us – revealed Himself to us—by His prophets and servants

Universal, Everlasting, Supreme

Power is universal, everlasting, supreme. This eternal Power keeps your heads above all waves and storms. It is strength; It is exalted; It will never be shaken.

Power Is Over All

Power of God is over all, goes over all, is spread over all. By the Power of God prophets are carried through and over all because the Lord's Seed and Power is over all. The universal Power of God goes over all apostasy and the Fall. over all.

Power Is Order

Fox lived in a time of great instability and disorder but he made a great effort to bring order to the Religious Society of Friends and to Friends themselves. He is interested in and believes in a God of order. Power is the Law and Order of Life and of the Gospel. This Power of the Lord God will order and keep down that which would be hasty or that which would be disobedient.

Power Is Life, Love and Dominion

Power is Life, habitation and dwelling. This Power brings from all the barren mountains, which are death, to the beginning, which is life; Life and immortality are brought to Light in Friends. So they should heed nothing but the Life and power of the Lord God, for all who are out of it will be confounded.

Power keeps over the world in cleanness and newness of life. So everyone should live and reign in the righteous Life and Power of God, doing the Truth to all.

Power is the Life that stands in God; It is Dominion.

Love is a characteristic of both the Lord God Almighty and of the Power of God. God Almighty is among us to do his will in his Love. so that we may be ordered to his glory.

> Never heed the raging waves of the sea, nor be troubled at his tongue that speaks nothing but tribulation, anguish and bondage, nor be troubled at the cords of the ungodly, for the cords of Love, the Power of God are stronger. (236)

There is safety in the God of Love and Power. He keep Friends to Himself and hears their cries and prayers. God Almighty be among you, to do his will in his Love and Unity.

Power Abolishes Death

Power abolishes death so neither death, grave nor all the powers are able to hold nor contain it. Possibly the most wonderful gift from Power is the promise of the Joy of everlasting fellowship with Him and of the Power of an endless life.

Power Takes Away the Occasion of All Wars

Fox sought to live in the power that takes away the occasion of all wars. Friends are to stand in the fear and dread of the lord God, his power, life, light, seed, and wisdom which take away the occasion of wars. They are to fight with spiritual weapons. While Friends stand in the Power of God who reigns, they will have victories over their enemies.

The God of Power Won't Tolerate Sin

The Power of God purges everything evil out of Friend's hearts and makes room for Himself. This Power will strike down the lust that causes pride so that understanding will grow clear and pure. For the Power of God was before unrighteousness and is a cross to it. Nonetheless some in the Fellowship are out of the Power of God.

God's Power is invisible and unlimited and brings down the carnal mind in Friends so the invisible and immortal things in them are brought to light.

The Power of God purges everything evil out of our hearts, tames and breaks all hasty spirits and make room for Himself.

But His Power can also be counted on to fight temptation, trouble and addiction.

> *Stand still in that which is pure, after you see yourselves, and Mercy comes in. After you see your thoughts and the temptations, do not think but submit to it, and the other will be hushed and gone. Then contentment comes When temptations and troubles appear, sink down in that which is pure, and all will be hushed and fly away. Your strength is to stand still. Stand still in that Power which brings peace.*
> *Letter 10, 1652*

(We see from this quote that Power is also peace and purity.)

Power of The Gospel

The Power of God is the Gospel and the Gospel expels that which burdens the soul.

The Power of God Is In the Meeting

Keep your meetings in the Power of God where you may know and feel the Power. In the Lord's Light, Power and Spirit meet together, and keep your meetings in the Name of Jesus Christ. The authority of the Meeting is the Power of Christ.

The Power seems also to be concerned with matters of little importance such as should Friends keep their hats on during meeting for worship, or not. Power also blasts those who oppose all forms, such as a set time for meeting. (One would hazard a guess that Power had a lot of help from G.F. in this regard.)

The Power of Darkness

Fox believes in a God of terrible power and tender love. Power is the name that he uses most often for God. Confident that God specially chose and shaped him, Fox believes that he has authority by the Power of God to judge, if he judges with the Spirit of Truth and by the Light. He also has the authority to understand the powers of darkness and to trample upon all this power and its authority. Prophets, particularly Jeremiah, were mocked, scoffed at and reproached for declaring against the sins and wickedness of their times. But by the Power of God t He was carried through and over all. (Fox frequently identifies with Jeremiah.)

The work that God has planned for Fox is to turn people "from the Power of Satan unto God." Fox believes that it is possible to fall out of God's Power and under the Power of Satan. For the Serpent's power tempts Eve to eat of the forbidden fruit, and she took and gives to her husband. So they fell under the power of darkness and out of the power of God which would have kept them in Dominion. Eve has knowledge and wisdom after the fall, but not in the Dominion in the power of God.

Friends should not fear the power of darkness for they have the bright morning Star in their hearts to expel it. All men and women's strength is in the power of God which goes over the power of darkness. They should be faithful in His Power having on the armor of Light which was before the power of darkness; they should walk in Righteousness and Holiness in the Power of God which goes over the power of darkness.

There is a summer religion, which appears when the sun shines, but when winter comes, religion and words are gone.

The religion—that is the Power of God—stands in that which was before the power of darkness.

Fox advises Friends not to "Let powers, principalities, prisons, thrones, nor dominions, spoiling your goods, mockings, scoffings, nor reproachings and pluckers of your hair separate you from the Love of God that you have in Christ Jesus, who conquered death and the devil and his power."

Friends are to follow the Lamb who reigns over all principalities and powers. The Lamb makes war in righteousness, and He will subdue all things to himself. He has the right to rule. Friends need not fear the devil with his beast's horns and heels for the Lamb will be victorious. The Lamb takes away human sin, breaks the devil's power over it. He will conquer the devil. He has power so Friends should follow Him and dwell in the Power of God in which they will be drawn up out of Satan's power. In the day of the Lamb's Power the church in her glory is appearing.

> *A Blessing: God Almighty, a God of Love, be with you all!*

Everyone Lives Within the God of Power

Fox believes that God lives within everyone and that it is possible to get in touch with this God within. But he also believes that everyone can get inside the God of Power! For Friends grow up in the Power, skip and leap in, and, as they are saints, have liberty in the Power, partake of It. But the best may be, identifying with Christ the Lamb, living and reigning in the Love, the righteous Life and Power of God doing the Truth to all.

Dwell in the power is a phrase that Fox uses often. Friends should all dwell
in the truth everyone according to their measures.
All they have to do is stand fast, stand still in that Power which brings peace; stand still in trouble and see the strength of the Lord. Wait in the Light to receive the Power to become Children of God. Everyone should walk in the Power and Spirit of God that is over all, allow It to have supremacy in their lives.

How Friends Should Behave Toward the Power

Friends are not to quench the spirit, nor abuse the Power but be faithful and obedient to it. They are not to add to It, nor take from It, but heed It, pay attention to It. They are to stir up others into Righteousness in the Power of God so that they may inherit this stable Power.

They are to rejoice, delight at the sound of the Power, sing His praises forever. They are to be valiant in the Power of God. But above all they must be careful not to be out the Power of God or lose It.

Friends are to follow the Lamb who reigns over all principalities and powers. The Lamb makes war in righteousness, and He will subdue all things to himself. He has the right to rule. Friends need not fear the devil with his beast's horns and heels for the Lamb will be victorious. The Lamb takes away human sin, breaks the devil's power over it. He will conquer the devil. He has power so Friends should follow Him and dwell in the Power of God in which they will be drawn up out of Satan's power. In the day of the Lamb's Power the church in her glory is appearing.

Fox also believes that each of us has authority from God to know this Power that shall never be shaken nor changed. We should answer the witness of God in everyone through this authority. We can also understand the power and authority of darkness. But the greatest gift is the Power of an endless life, to live with God forever.

The name Almighty shows God's power over all. This Lord God Almighty will be with us and keep us turned to the Creator to worship and serve Him.

> O happy day! PRAISES! Praises! PRAISE you the Lord, you righteous ones, sing PRAISES to the Lord God Almighty forever. Letter 38, 1653

King

> *King, immortal, invisible, the only wise God, blessed forever. Amen. Letter 339, 1677*

During George Fox's lifetime, the king is a man with supreme political power and authority. But God is not just a King. He is the King of kings, His power and authority are greater than any power on earth. Many years ago when an atomic bomb was exploded in New Mexico as a test, every clergyman worth his salt preached, the next Sunday, on how God was more powerful than any atomic bomb. Fox is doing a similar thing here for a king was the most powerful individual he knows. This King of kings and Lord of Lords, this powerful, all sufficient God is also the true shepherd who protects the lambs from dogs. He feeds them in green pastures and gives life abundantly.

Invisible Lord, Invisible Power. God is spirit and can't be seen with the human eye. Fox knows that God is radically different from himself; the word invisible sums this up. Other words, that show how radically different God is from us, are holy, numinous, other. Glorious and wondrous show the resplendent and awe inspiring nature of God.

"God who is invisible, by his invisible power and spirit, brings down the carnal mind in you, so the invisible and immortal things in you are brought to light."

Immortal means that God had no beginning and will have no end; God will never die. For God, eternal and everlasting mean always, forever, evermore, perpetual, time without measure, enduring through all time; for us, eternity is to be with God forever.

The God of Order

The living eternal God of Truth is Order; walk in it and it have joy, peace and comfort. Fox believes that all God's children should live in His Light and Spirit for He gives them the gifts of Grace and Faith. By the Wisdom of God were all things made; by the wisdom of God must all things be ordered again to His Glory.

Blessed is the man or woman that delights in the Law and Order of Love, the Law and Order of Faith, the Law and Order of Life and of the Gospel, the Power of God. Letter 361, 1679

God is Yes

God is Yes, affirmation. Fox has a positive, vision of God and even though he knows that he is a sinner, he doesn't wallow in sin. He believes that God's love heals and makes him whole.

Universal

The Powerful Father is universal and everlasting. Letter 184, 1659

A Universal God is One who is knowable to all persons. God pours out His Spirit on all men and women, young and old, rich and poor, with dark or light colored skin so that all may know and worship Him. Fox is convinced that everyone can know the Light and Spirit of God within. His Power is universal, everlasting, supreme. Writing in letter 217, 1662 we see Fox at his universal best: Spread Truth abroad to both Jews, Christians and Heathens. For all people – Jews, Christians, and Heathens – can know and love God and spend eternity in His Kingdom. They will all share the Peace, Life, Joy, dominion and prosperity.

THE LIGHT

I saw that there was an ocean of death; but an infinite ocean of light and love, which flowed over the ocean of darkness. The Journal, 1647

The First Principle of Pure Religion.

The purpose of the Fox's Catechism for Children is that "they may come to learn of Christ, the Light, the Truth, the Way, that leads to know the Father, the God of all Truth." Although the format – questions and answers – is conventional, the Catechism for Children is not. Principally it is a defense of the central belief of Friends: Christ Jesus saith, I am the way who doth enlighten every man that cometh into the world, and no man cometh to the Father but by me, ever man having a light from Christ the way, it leads to the Father.

The Light is God. Through the Light we see Him in all His Glory. The Light is Christ. Christ's true and best name is Light. The first principle of pure religion is that Christ Jesus is the way who enlightens every man and woman who come into the world. The Light is not of this world – being immortal and eternal– but comes from the Father who made the world. Everyone, having a light from Christ the way, is led to the Father of Light. Believers, saints, Friends are able to see Christ through the Light, love our neighbor who is also enlightened with the same Light All we have to do is be still in the Light who discovers all things – ways, words, actions, thoughts – and demonstrates them. In the Light we see Christ, the way to the

Father of Light, the source of Light. (No one comes to the Father but by Him.) In the Light, we see God in His Glory.

The Light has power. Friends may know the Light and taste His Power for the Light and the Power of God make an end to all unholiness.

Christ Is the Light of the World

Although the Light is many things to Fox, primarily He is Christ. Christ will enlighten us, give us understanding. He is the way, life and wisdom from above, the Author of our living Faith. He gives us faith Heb.12.2. 84 and brings 85 us in oneness through one Faith. Col.1.18. He understands all ways, sees before there were many faiths to His one true faith.

The Light, restorer and seeker of the lost, binder up of the broken, mediates between God and man, reconciles us to God and justifies us to Him. ("Justifies us to God." Fox's language is precise. If he writes that the Light justifies us to God that is what he means.) The Light is the first step to peace who gives us peace.

The True Light, spiritual and eternal, by whom the world was made, is glorified with the Father.

Own the Light

We must own the Light that shines in our hearts. (Own means to confess, acknowledge, be aware of the Light.) For He lives in us, helps us, shows us what is right and wrong, gives us the knowledge of the Glory of God in the Face of Jesus Christ. We are obedient to Him. Some men and women turn away from knowledge and wisdom because they do not own the Light.

The self doesn't own the Light. Self may mean an individual's essential being that distinguishes him or her from others. However, Fox uses the word here in the sense of being self-centered, preoccupied with oneself and one's affairs. Self absorbed persons don't follow Christ, don't own the Light, but instead act as if they possess it, try to tell the Light what to do.

Brand New

There is a New covenant, priesthood, temple, living way. This Light that we have from the covenant of Light lets us see whatever separates us from God. The New covenant of Light is an everlasting covenant. But above all the Light of Christ makes everything new. The idea of all things becoming brand new, starting over, is an appealing one.

The Law, the First Covenant and the Old Testament made nothing perfect. But the Light fulfills the Law and the Prophets. Now the Law is the Light, and the testimony of Jesus is the Spirit of prophesy. All we have to do is to wait in the Light to inherit the promise.

The Church

The Church is in God, the Light, Christ Jesus the Savior of the Soul, the Rock upon whom it is built. He is its Head. The Church is not an invention, a creation of something in the mind of man; it is not a great house but a pillar and ground of the Truth.

Fox asks the question: How shall a company of people, who are full of pride, deceit and blemishes, spots and wrinkles, come to God's Church? He makes hard things sound easy.

For everyone has a Light from Christ Jesus and is turned to the Light, so we are turned to the Church.

He very definitely believes that many sects and opinions, many ways, many teachings, many worships are not in the Spirit and in the Light, who is Truth. These opinions and judgments are out where the prince of darkness and of the air, where the distractions and confusions are; they are not with the Light, Prince of Peace, Prince of Life.

How can all this be healed? We must be brought to the power that answers the principle of God in all, the Light who is Jesus Christ who has enlightened us even though we have sinned. Thus, through the power the Gospel, life and Immortality, we may come to light.

Predestination

Fox is a Universalist, not a predestinarian. He believes that everyone can know God the Light and be saved by Him, not that we are preordained to heaven or hell. During his lifetime the doctrine of predestination is associated mainly with Calvinists but many believe it.

His harsh language against Professors, Teachers, Christians who do not believe in the Light and who are filled with unrighteous pride, ambition, covetousness, wickedness, and ungodliness, seems not to be about predestination but to say that their religion is just a pretense and not the Truth. It is made by the will of man, not the will of God. The crux of the matter is that Preachers, Teachers and Professors do not believe the central tenet of the Quaker faith, that Christ enlightens every man that comes into the world.

He contrasts the behavior of Professors and Teachers with God's righteousness, His Son, His Holy Prophets and Saints. They understand and believe the Apostles' words about Christ enlightening and saving everyone. Fox believes that no one else holds this belief in the Light in its true form and no one has done so since the time of the Apostles.

AN ABC FOR GROWNUPS ABOUT THE LIGHT

ABIDE in the Light of Christ. ALL must be turned to the Light.
BELIEVE in the Light. Be BOLD in the Light for He BRINGS us to Christ.
The Light is COMFORT, wisdom, love and mercy.
DWELL, wait, walk in the Light for He leads to the DAY dawning and the DAY Star arising in our hearts.
The Light is EVERYWHERE and in EVERYONE. So all people have EQUALITY.
The Light, FOUNTAIN of Life. FORGIVE each other in the Light.
The Light is GOD; He is GLORIOUS.
The Light is a Heavenly Light, a Heavenly Treasure within; He HAMMERS down, judges evil.
The Light is INTIMATE and personal; the Light is our INWARD teacher.
Dwelling in the Light, which is unchangeable, we come to JUDGE all the changeable ways and worships. The JUST walk in a path which is a shining light.
The Light will KEEP our minds turned toward God.
In the Light we receive the Love of God; Those that LOVE the Light receive LIFE.
The Light is a MYSTERY.
We do NOT own the Light.
The Light is ONE; He is the same always. So we must OBEY the Light.
The Light is PURE.
The Light changes QUARRELS to peace.
The Light shows us what is RIGHT.
The Light, the SUM and SUBSTANCE.
The Light is TRUTH and UNITY.
All people are VALUABLE because the Light lives WITHIN us.

> We are eXhorted to Live in the Light. We must eXperience the Light for ourselves.
> The Light is in the YEARLY Meeting.
> The Light is in the ZENITH and the nadir.

Who Is This Light In Whom We Must Believe?

Everyone must believe in the Light. This belief brings peace and gives victory. None comes to be children of the Light but such as believe in the Light. Fox describes the Light as a heavenly Light, a divine Light, a saving Light, a Heavenly Treasure within and the Light of the Glory of God. In the Light we receive the love of God. We should be content in the Light for the He is comfort, wisdom, love and mercy. The Light is pure, sufficient. The Light is spiritual but He gives material support as well. He will clothe us if we love and obey Him.

There are not individual Lights; the Light is one. The Light is consistent, doesn't differ in different persons, male or female, young or old. Always the same, He doesn't differ throughout time. The Light understands the world. The Light is given to all, even to unbelievers, we don't own Him.

Dwell In the Light Within

The Light is within us. He is with us everywhere no matter where we are or whom we are with. We should love the Light within. When writing of our relationship with the Light, Fox uses phrases like turn to the Light, wait in the Light, walk in the Light, stand still in the Light, dwell in the Light. We walk in the Light and have fellowship with the Son and the Father and fellowship with one another. We stand still in the Light, who comes from the Word. We wait in the Light who turns us to holiness For if we dwell in the Light, we will receive eternal Life. All we have to do is love the Light and wait. God does the rest.

Fox believes that the Light is in the Meeting for worship. The mystical nature of the Meeting, the sacred nature of the

Meeting, the importance of the Meeting are all due to the presence of the Light, Christ.

The Light Calls Us to Repentance

The Light calls us to repentance. He shows us what is right and what is wrong, distinguishes the precious from the vile. He will show us our lives, how we have acted, whom we have hurt. If there is strife among Friends the Light will judge and condemn it. So we should heed the Light for He will show us what is contrary. .

The Light sets a watch over all our thoughts, words, and actions. He also helps us so that we can change, and will give us the strength, the courage to give up whatever we are doing wrong. Secretly, the Light will lead us out of darkness. (For Fox light and the day are good while darkness and night are evil.) If we speak, think, or act in any way that is against God, the Light will reprove us. But especially, He will lead us from loving and worshiping ourselves and caring only for bodily comforts, to the worship of God.

The unjust person, who can neither see nor abide the Light, calls Him natural, created, made or conscience. But the Light is not our conscience; He is in our conscience. (Fox is not entirely consistent in this but he does write, "Mind the light of God in your consciences which will show you all deceit.")

Belief in the Light within means that all people are valuable, so there should be equality for all.

The Light is not some indulgent grandfather. The Light condemns, shows sin, evil and lust; the Light keeps us chaste. But it is possible to lose the Light. The Light is the Kingdom of heaven and enables us to see this Kingdom. If we go from the Light, we go from the Kingdom, Power, Life, Glory. In the Light we see our unrighteousness, for the Light is the eye. But if the eye comes to be closed, then the testimony of Christ is not received and the Light is gone. The Light of the wicked is put out.

The antichrist is blind to the Light, denies the Light, is against the Light, goes from the Light which enlightens him, does not confess Christ the Light.

It is possible to lose the Light. For the Light condemns and the Light of the wicked is put out. But He also saves us from this sin; He breaks our bonds of iniquity. ("Breaking our bonds" is a phrase that Fox uses often based on his experience of courts and prison.) Those that are out of the Light are unable to pray; those that vex the Spirit and quench it cannot pray to God.

Drunks are out of the Light, out of the fear of God. "They devour the Creation upon their lusts."

Wars and Quarrels

The Light leads us out of the occasion of wars and out of wars themselves. He casts out quarrelsome spirits and leads into true peace. The Light is also Power. This power will shake the earth and remove it out of its place.

The Light Inspired the Bible

George Fox knows the Bible, or, as he calls it, the Scriptures, very well and he was deeply influenced by it. His writings are filled with direct quotes and allusions to it. The Light inspired the scriptures and now helps us understand them. It distinguishes the true prophet's word from the false, the words of holy men from the words of unholy ones. But the Bible is only a declaration of the fountain, not the fountain itself. Fox will give a long and elaborate biblical argument for a certain premise. Then he will say something to the effect that Christ is sufficient.

Unity Purity and Truth

Unity, purity and truth are words that George Fox uses often to describe the Light. If we come to conclusions based on human reasoning, and if we try to dominate others, this is wrong. We should express only what the Light reveals to us. Then we will say what is right and there will be no dissension, just true unity.

The Light is God, Creator, glorified; He is Christ, Truth, purity. Universal; everywhere, within all persons, throughout time and before time. He fills all space, has no beginning and will have no end. But He is also intimate, personal, direct, positive, and above all immediate. The Light can be addressed and responded to; it is possible to experience the Light first hand, without an intermediary.

A person of great faith, Fox has a deep commitment and holds himself accountable for his actions. In his letters which span many years, we see the fruits of his long experience in the faith. It is a rare person who can express their faith as well as he does. The Light is Christ, the Light is God, the Light is everywhere, everyone possesses Him and the Light is in our conscience showing us what to do. There is no question but that Fox experiences the Light. The great pleasure of reading his letters is to share the wonderful, immediate, personal, loving Light whom he knows. He has a confidence, a sureness about God so that reading his pastoral letters gives the reader confidence, too.

But Fox has certain givens that do not necessarily characterize Friends today. He takes it for granted that we will be devout, believing, orthodox Christians and that this is the better part of our religious experience. He also assumes that we know the Bible intimately and accept that it – through our experience and the Holy Spirit – has a special kind of authority.

> *A Blessing: Dear hearts, hearken to the Light to be guided by Him. For if you love the Light, you love Christ. In the Name of the Lord Jesus Christ consider it. The Lord open your understandings to know Him!* Letter 17, 1652

CREATOR, THE LIVING GOD, LIFE, FATHER OF LIFE

God is the creator of the universe and this creation reveals His incredible power. But Fox just mentions in passing the creation of the world, how God divided the great sea from the land and the light from the darkness. What really interests him is that creation continues each day. God is interested in, and involved in, these day to day changes. He causes the snow to melt and the rain to water the plants. This Creator is a Living God – Fox also calls Him the Living Light – brings spring each year with new plants and grass. He causes the trees and crops to grow and makes the fishes of the sea breathe and live. An especially nice touch is that Fox writes that God created the sun just to warm us when we are cold. This Living God is to be worshiped. This may sound complicated but as always Fox makes it easy. All we have to do is be babes of God and wait for the living food from the living God. This will nourish us up to eternal life.

Fox does not believe that the world never changes. He sees a world in which change takes place every day. God is involved in these day to day changes.

Fox calls the Creator, the Living God, Father of Life. The Father of Life lives, reigns, and rules amongst His gardens. He also uses homey, comfortable, everyday sorts of names for Him: the Heavenly Seedman and the Heavenly husbandman who lives amongst his gardens, vineyards, and plants. God waters us with His blessing. This Living God gives us breath, life and strength and nourishes the tender plant in us, that we may bring forth fruits of righteousness unto Him. 231

It has never been more beautifully written that God is right here with us constantly. He lives and rules among us, not only giving us Life, but giving us the increase of Life.

Blessing: Dwell in love in your hearts to God and to one another! The work and harvest of the Lord is great. My prayers to God for you are that you may be faithful in the work.
Letter 18, 1652: Be Faithful in the Work

An ABC for Grownups about Working in the Garden of God

All believe and live as the family of God, in Truth, ATOP of all the mountains and hills.
The Lord, with His Eternal ARM and Power, preserve you in the service in his Vineyard. Glory be to His name forever.

The Light is a BROOM, made of a bundle of twigs, which will cleanse your heart and mind. *CUT* up the roots with your heavenly axe, for the DAY of harvest is known. The Lord God waters His pastures with His heavenly DEW, making them fruitful.

May EVERLASTING life be the FRUIT of your holiness.

Thou has a FINE compass. So in the Seed spread the Truth over your part of the World. For the Lord has a vine and a mountain to be set up that-a-ways and a standard and ensign held out to other nations. The Lord God Almighty preserve thee!

Bring forth fresh GREEN fruit to the praise and Glory of God., being GRAFTED into the GREEN tree that never withers.

Some are GATHERING, some HARROWING their Seed of Life. With integrity and joy, kindle the Light according to your measure.

Let your faith stand in the Lord's power, which is your HEDGE and will keep you safe.

All men and women are to labor in the Garden of God so that we may be redeemed up into His IMAGE.

When we find ourselves being JANGLERS, grumbling, whining, wrangling people, we should go out and work in the garden for awhile.

The KERNEL is found within; the husk is without, which the swine feed upon. But the pearl is hid from them and they would devour them in whom the pearl is found.

Everyone may keep their own lily in their own garden; which LILY does exceed Solomon in all his glory.

The MOUNTAIN of the Lord is always green, with fresh springs and fruit; those who live under His teaching know it.

Live in the Life of God and be NURSERS of His plants.

Dwell everyone of you under your OWN Vine and seek not to be great.

For God is ORDER and PAYS the PLOWMAN his wages of a heavenly PENNY.
Mind God's PLANTATIONS that his Lilies and Vines may grow and bring forth Fruit to his Praise, who gives the increase.

God is the QUICKENER; He renews all life.

Don't think about the winter and cold weather, nor the long night, for the ROSES grow and the gardens give a good smell.

Reapers collect the SPIRITUAL truth which flourishes as the rose, the heavenly treasure. Under your own vine, none will make you afraid.

Fellow laborers in the Truth, who are subduing the earth, its knowledge, its carnal wisdom and beating down and THRESHING in hope of getting forth the wheat.

Live in the Seed, which was before enmity was, and you will feel UNITY, Virtue and Peace.

The Lord, with his eternal Arm and Power, preserve you in the service in his VINEYARD. Glory to His name forever.

Sit under your own VINE and you will bring forth fruit to God abundantly. Be not afraid.

The thresher has gotten the WHEAT out of the sheaf, the heavenly wheat, with his heavenly flail. This fruit of the earth shall be excellent.

E*X*cellent old women and YOUNG men labor in the vineyards that everyone of you may have his penny.

Take upon you Christ's YOKE, and with his heavenly plough, turn up the earth which has oppressed and grieved the tender Seed.

Be ZEALOUS of the work in God's garden.

Working in God's Garden

George Fox uses the imagery of plants, gardening and nature to give a vivid picture of God the Creator and of our part in creation, working in His garden. We must dress it and be preserved in His wisdom, for the work and harvest are great. Faithful servants laboring in love, some threshing, some ploughing, some keeping the sheep. Others harrow their Seed of Life, according to their measure. The thresher has gotten the wheat out of the sheaf, the heavenly wheat, with his heavenly flail.

Fox genuinely believes that everlasting life will be the fruit of our holiness.

He advises us not to think about the winter and cold weather. Instead remember that the sun shines and the Light is clear and not dim, that we may see our way, even though there is a stormy tempest in the sea. We should mind the summer and the singing of the birds, not the winter and night, in which the beasts do yell. (Fox often sets up dichotomies to set good and evil, right and wrong in sharp contrast.)

We are to grow up in the inner man as trees of righteousness which the Lord has planted, growing in wisdom and understanding of the will of God. If we wait upon the Lord, He will perfect his work amongst us. For Christ is the Green Tree which never withers, into whom we are grafted by belief in the Light. As grafts, we are nourished with heavenly loving nourishment.

Fox can be a two-hundred percenter, a twenty-four hourer. He often asks such hard things of us. But he can also give us a thing that is doable: Be as a pleasant orchard to the Holy God.

An orchard is beautiful – a cherry tree in blossom and then in fruit – productive, useful, practical, needful. An orchard is generous. Even a small orchard will produce more fruit than an individual or a family can eat so the abundance may be shared with others. Be a pleasant orchard. Pleasant is nice, agreeable, charming. It is possible to be charming for the Lord, to be useful, practical, productive, to be a tree laden with fruit. This is something that can be done. Anyone can be a pleasant orchard for the Lord.

> *My prayers to God are that you may be faithful in the work.* George Fox, 1652

GOD OF UNLIMITED LOVE

The God in whom Fox believes is not just a God of Love but a God of unlimited love. This love is pure and peaceable. Friends should dwell in it in unity of the Spirit for it warms our hearts and unites us together. If we do this, we will be able to look above all outward suffering and dwell in that which is above all and will stand when all other is gone. This Love enables us to bear all things; whatever wicked men do to us, or what God may try us with. For His Love casts out false fear, unites the hearts of His people together in heavenly joy, concord and unity. Mind the "pure Refreshings in the unlimited Love of God," For God preserves us by his eternal arm, carries us in his hand and opens his ears to the cries of those who suffer.

Love Overcomes and Never Fails

Dear Friends and brethren in Christ Jesus, all walk in the Power and Spirit of God, that is over all, in Love and Unity. For Love overcomes and Love and Charity never fails, but casts out false fear, is of God and unites all the hearts of his people together in heavenly Joy, concord and Unity.   Amen
Letter 417 written in London, the 27th of the 5th Month, 1689.

In Letter 417, Fox defines God's love. It preserves, overcomes, never fails, unites. He seems to be remembering I John 4:18 when he writes love, "casts out false fears." This is the fear of the opinion of others, especially those who disapprove of our love of God.

How is it possible to take advantage of God's love, His providence? God's plan for every person is that we are to love Him and to do His will in their lives so that we will spend eternity loving Him. We must start right now, must experience God for themselves. It is possible to know about God because He has told us about Himself. That's what revelation means?

What has God revealed about Himself? First, there is a God. Second, He made the world and everything in it, creating us in His Image. He loves us and has a plan for our lives. One way in which we are made in the Image of God is that we can love Him in return. We need to love God but can't love someone we don't know. For real love to exist there must be some reciprocal action. God loves us, and we love God in return.

It is easier to think of God as merciful, not just; it is much more comfortable to dwell on God's kindness, generosity and love than it is to think of his justice. But Fox knows God as a God who loves the righteous; one who punishes the disobedient.

God shows holy love and holy anger; both mercy and justice are characteristics of God. He shows His mercy in kindness and pity; He spares and forgives us when we break His laws. Justice means dealing fairly and equitably with us. We are held accountable and responsible for what we do.

A Blessing: May the God of power keep you in His unlimited love, all one family of love, children of one father and of the household of God.

AN ABC FOR GROWNUPS ABOUT THE GOD OF LOVE

God's Love

is A-TOP the mountains and hills eternal arm.

is a BLESSING, makes it possible to BEAR all things.   Letter 234 p 195

Never heed the CORDS of the ungodly, for the CORDS of love are stronger. Letter 236, 1664

DWELL in the Love that can bear all things. Letter 400, 1685

The God of Life, Peace and ENDLESS Love be with you all and clothe you with the garment of EVERLASTING   praise. Letter 213, 1661

FELLOWSHIP in the everlasting

GLORIOUS

HEAVENLY and HOLY

INFINITE

JOYFUL

KINDLY

LONG suffering

MERCIFUL

NEVER fails

OVER all; OVERCOMES evil

PEACEFUL, PRESERVES

never QUENCHES

RECONCILIATION, REDEMPTION

SANCTIFYING

TRUE, TENDER

UNIVERSAL, UNITES in Heavenly Joy

VICTORIOUS

WONDROUS

eXtravagant

YES

Blessing: To God be all honor, glory, dominion, praise, and thanksgiving both now and forevermore.

GOD OF PEACE

God, who is love, is the author of Peace, not strife and confusion. Letter 4, 1651

Blessed are those whose minds are stayed upon the Lord, for they shall be kept in perfect peace ... for it is a whole Peace, which cannot be broken. So here is not only a perfect Peace, but a blessing which comes from the God of all Peace. Letter 249, 1667

Fox never writes anything once when he can write it several times. But it is always worth repeating especially here for peace is whole, perfect and a blessing. We are heirs of the God of Peace so we can walk in Peace with Him and with one another. We have the promise of everlasting peace, which comes from the mountain, so we can stand fast in Him and He will keep us. The God of Life, Peace and endless Love is with us all and clothes us with the garment of everlasting praise.

The name of the eternal exalted God is Peace. The Father of peace, the Heavenly Teacher of Peace creates us in His Image and fills our hearts with love, life, mercy and joy. (Because we are created in His Image we can live peaceful lives.) Grace and Peace are ours in abundance so that we will be complete in everything good

God brings peace to all nations and all people so that all people of the earth may enjoy peace, which flows as a river from the

Rock and Foundation of Life. (God gave us His Son, the King of Peace, the Prince of Life. Such a Peace the world cannot take away. Christ joins God in bringing peace to everyone.) Peace is order; no Peace is chaos. God who is Order, not vengeance, fills our hearts with wisdom so that we may be at Peace among ourselves. God gives us Peace and unity.

Over and over again Fox writes in the pastoral letters that Friends should get along with each other. There should be peace in Meeting. God's everlasting Kingdom is above all strife.

Peace is sometimes quiet, sometimes jubilant. It restores and reconciles all things; it is safety and sanctuary. Truth is peaceable.

Quoting Romans 15: 13: The Lord of Hosts said, "In this place I will give Peace.

A Benediction: Depart in Peace for a harvest of righteousness is sown for those who make Peace. God give us an everlasting Peace

THE QUAKER PEACE TESTIMONY

George Fox left an heritage of witnessing for peace – the witness for peace is just about the only thing that Friends agree on today – which has been a source of inspiration to Friends through the centuries. Friends' duty, our job, is to keep the Peace of the Prince of princes. The spirit of Christ leads into all Truth and never asks any one to make war. The peace testimony tries to build trust between people and nations. The Peace testimony has found expression as conscientious objection, disarmament and relief work for victims of war. Quakers have been particularly concerned for children caught in the midst of war. Fox's belief in universality, brotherhood of all people, is demonstrated in the peace testimony. Friends should guard against placing their dependence on fleets and armies. Instead they should pray to the Father of the Universe that He breathe the spirit of reconciliation into the hearts of his erring and contending creatures. The human family is one, children of one Father. How can anyone war against the members of one's own family? Fox believes in the worth of all persons; war is the most terrible destroyer of this worth.

Pure, perfect peace." What a wonderful phrase! Only George Fox could have written it. A Quaker Community Peace Resource Organization (PRO) helps individuals find this pure perfect peace. Organizations of this kind looks for peaceful solutions to conflict, helps individuals who are concerned about how violent our society has become to do something constructive about violence. As communities grow and compete for the same resources, violence instead of peace often is the result. Our children and grandchildren are exposed to violence continually through TV, movies and our own example The example of goodness, courtesy and peace are needed so children can learn peace as an alternative to violence.

A PRO discovers individuals who know how to live in a peaceful way and who are able to teach others in this lifestyle. Peace is a skill to be learned. These peace workers, in turn, train others. Soon there are sufficient trained workers so that peaceful behavior is a viable alternative to violent behavior. The whole community unlearns violence and learns peace. If all the peaceful people and resources available in a community are brought together, and made easily available and affordable, then people will consider peaceful alternatives to violence.

A community can support peace by making information available about peaceful alternatives to violence. They can also organize workshops, conferences, vigils, delegations and coalitions. They may provide an unarmed visible presence in time of unrest. Possibly the most successful means of peaceful intervention are prayers, negotiations, and off-the-record-meetings. The use of mediation and arbitration in courtrooms is being used more often.

Inspired by Fox, some Friends see a life based on non-violence as an ideal. United Nations peace-keeping operations are an attempt at non-violence on a military level. These peace keepers act as family friends who have moved into a household stricken by disaster. They try to help without destroying the family. Instead of might making right, the UN works through peaceful means, mediation, law, covenants and treaties.

Just as there is conflict in the family, there is conflict in the world. The "world's people," like the members of a family, must learn peaceful ways of settling conflict. The dignity and worth of all people is a cornerstone of the UN. This organization works to improve the lot of women around the world. Quakers believe that women should have equal opportunity along with men to use the gifts that God has given them.

UN efforts at sustainable development provide practical help to poor communities. Sustainable development links peace, the economy, the environment and society. This approach has much in common with the ideas of John Woolman, eighteenth century Quaker mystic and social reformer, who writes about the connection of the loss of soil fertility, the price of grain and the exploitation of the poor. The UN seems to agree with him that people should try to feed themselves first instead of exporting food needed at home. The UN has high ideals but sometimes the day to day reality doesn't meet them. However, if you don't have ideals to aspire too, nothing will be accomplished.

At the Friends World Conference and Consultation (FWCC) meeting in New Zealand in 2004, a delegate, a man, from Africa tells of their commitment to spread peace and to find peaceful resolutions to conflict. They want especially to respect the human rights of women and children and stop social discrimination in all activities. They also want to respect both public and private property. They would never join political parties or associations that seek to use war to meet their ends; they would remove themselves from armed groups.

GEORGE FOX'S ATTITUDE TOWARD WAR

George Fox defines his position on violence and how Friends are to deal with it in Letter 215 written in 1662.

> Live in Christ and bear fruit to glorify God.
>
> Live in the Truth. Be faithful and valiant in it.
>
>> By which you may see over that which stains, corrupts, cankers, loads and burdens the creation. By which Power of God and Truth you may answer the Spirit of God in all.
>
> Be tender to one another for that is the least love.
>
> Let your backs and cheeks be ready to the smiters. Fear not suffering; fear not him that can kill the body only, but can't hurt the soul; fear not him who can spoil your goods.
>
> Let your patience be perfect for it is the Good that overcomes the evil; the Lamb Christ is Victorious.

The Declaration of 1660 to Charles II: A Declaration from the harmless and innocent people of God, called Quakers, against all sedition, plotters, and fighters in the world for removing the ground of jealousy and suspicion from magistrates and people concerning wars and fightings.

The Declaration to Charles II – written by Fox and others and presented to the King on the 21st day of the 11th Month, 1660 - sets the standard for the Quaker peace testimony. It documents Fox's position on all violence. "We do utterly deny all outward wars, and strife, and fightings with outward weapons, for any end and this is our testimony to the whole world. Friends are to seek peace, to be righteous, to know God, to provide for the welfare of others and to encourage peace for all.

Fox wanted to set Friends apart from those suspected of plotting to overthrow the established authorities.

> Friends had not hurt any person nor stolen their possessions.
> Friends had not plotted against anyone, nor had they incited any rebellion against the king.
> Friends had not retaliated, when others wronged them,.
> Friends had not resisted the authority of legitimate government officials except when it is for conscience' sake.

War Is Sinful

The epistle of James, chapter four verses 1-3, gives men's lusts as the origin of war

> From whence come wars and fightings among you? Come they not hence, even of your lusts that war in your members?

2 Ye lust, and have not: ye kill, and desire to have, and cannot obtain: ye fight and war, yet ye have not, because ye ask not.
3 Ye ask, and receive not, because ye ask amiss, that ye may consume it upon your lusts.

Fox believes that Friends experience of the Lamb Christ makes these lusts irrelevant. He writes: I live in the virtue of that life and power that takes away the occasion of all wars. He denied all outward war. There is no good war, no just war. He would not fight in an outward war with material weapons. However, he would fight in an inner spiritual war—the Lamb's war —with spiritual weapons.

THE LAMB

And so in Him be faithful, who is your crown. Let no man take your crown from you. Yea, I say, be faithful to him, who was the Lamb slain from the foundation of the world," (Rev. 13:8) who reigns and sits down at the right hand of God, till all his enemies be made his footstool. Letter231, 1663 Fox seems to give the Lamb Christ an extra bit of Power for He makes war in righteousness and will rule, subdue, conquer and be victorious over human sin and the power of the devil. Fox doesn't think that it a mystery that the Lamb should have victory over all the wild, uncontrollable, the wolfish part of human nature, for He is clean and holy. He has the right to rule. Friends need not fear the devil with his Beast's Horns and Heels for the Lamb will be victorious over the Wild Beasts. He writes Beast with a capital B when he means the devil; he uses a small b to denote the uncontrollable part of human nature. The Lamb takes away human sin and breaks the devil's power over it. The Lamb will plague the beast. The Lamb is order; the devil is disorder.

The Lamb is the special defender of Friends under persecution. So all thanks be to Him, who is come to rule alone in his saints. The righteous should rejoice for the Lamb is victorious over the beast that pushed at Him. Friends have both the Power of God and the Power of the Lamb Christ to defend and help them. So they should not fear suffering for Christ suffered. They should let their backs and cheeks be ready to the "smiters." They should not fear him that can kill the body only, but can't hurt the soul. In this way they will be preserved in gentleness and in boldness by the Lord God Almighty.

Friends have been tried by goods spoiling, by bonds, by whippings, by "mockings" and reproach. Some have been tried unto death and have proved to be pure gold that comes forth brighter and brighter. Fox has great concern for Friends so he writes to them in Letter 192,1660 with great tenderness: From a lover of your soul's eternal Good, and of your establishment in Righteousness and Peace in this day of the Lamb's Power, Glory to the Highest forever!
Fox advises Friends to follow the Lamb, Christ, King, Prince, Royal Seed, who reigns over all principalities and powers. (Principalities and powers are angelic beings, often evil ones.) The Lamb makes war in righteousness, and He will subdue all things to himself.

As always for Fox, Christ is the answer. He tells all "dear friends and brethren in the world" that they should be of good cheer for Christ has overcome the world. In Him they will overcome the devil and his works, and without Him they can do nothing. Nevertheless through His power and strength, they will be able to do all things.

Suffering, Persecution, Imprisonment

> All dear Friends everywhere, who have no helper but the Lord, who is your Strength and your Life, let your cries and prayers be to Him who with his eternal Power has kept your heads above all waves and storms. Let none, whose habitation is in the Lord, go out in the stormy time of the night. Letter 280, 1670

Fox maintained that Friends are persecuted for their worship. In Letter 238, 1664, he writes, "They can find no occasion against you except that you worship God in spirit and obey the commands of Christ Jesus." Then he makes it very personal because Christ is our Friend, and He has a "fellow feeling" with us. When Friends are suspected of making war, it is without any evidence. But Friends shouldn't be surprised or overwhelmed by this. The Lamb suffered; the Godly must also suffer. We shows our love for Christ by sharing His sufferings. Saints, Friends, will see the end of all wars but they must suffer first.

Friends should be confident for God will lay no more on them than they can bear. Those who suffer gain the victory which brings in the eternal covenant of Christ's peace. They must have patience, love God and one another. For the God of Peace supports and strengthens them through all their sufferings so that He may be glorified.

When forcibly attacked, Fox always allowed his attackers to do their worst. He expected the same of Friends. They are not only to accept beatings but joyfully receive fetters, irons and stripes. Suffering is a gift of God. Undaunted by violence, Friends are to be bold and courageous for the Truth. All this evil is transitory; God will overcome it. Prison and outward bonds have an end; the Lamb is eternal. All prophets, apostles and martyrs are tested; Friends should rejoice in their suffering.

> Dear Friends: Those that live godly in Christ Jesus must suffer persecution. God is righteous, God is pure, holy and just. God is clean. He that is godly and holy, suffers by the ungodly, unrighteous, unclean, unjust and filthy. And so, the just suffers by the unjust. He

> that is born of the flesh, persecutes him that is born of the Spirit.   Letter 8, 1652

Men and women, young and old suffered, beaten, abused and imprisoned. They suffered for not swearing allegiance to the king, "not giving the world's compliments and their honor," and not raising their hats to their social superiors. Possessions and means of livelihood confiscated on the word of paid informers. Friends are not allowed to hold Meetings for Worship. The law of Praemunire, described above in the chapter on *George Fox's Time*, is revived to deal with those persons who refuse the oath of allegiance.

Comforting Friends in prison, Fox reminded them that the Lamb Christ will never forsake them. He is the strong tower in whom those who are persecuted and suffer may find refuge. Christ suffers right along with them. Persecution is the trial of their faith. Then, he writes in letter 226, 1663, "Dear Friends keep low for there is no danger." The Lamb is your protector so even if things look bad, you are all right.

What Can Friends Do To Help Themselves?

With perfect patience and minding God's power, Friends should have faith in the Lamb who will be victorious. Fox did not want Friends to be involved in war; he did not want there to be any strife among us. Instead we are to know the spirit which preaches peace by the Lamb. Fear him who can spoil our goods for the "fleece will grow again." However, Fox has practical advice for Friends on confronting their persecutors and presenting their case in court.

Friends should keep a copy of all their sufferings and the names of their persecutors. When served with writs (for example not paying tithes), copies should be made for presenting in court. Those who are beaten or wounded when going to meeting, and those who are bruised in meeting or taken out of meeting should make copies and have them witnessed by two or three who saw the events take place. These documents should be either taken to court or sent to the king. In this way, the persecuted can keep a-top of those who wish them evil. The same procedure is to be followed for not giving money to rebuild Anglican churches. Fox did not avoid confrontation and advised Friends to confront their persecutors.

Although Friends cannot count on being treated fairly, we should organize our defense in the county. Any persecutions from justices, constables and bailiffs should be written down, signed, and witnessed and presented to the judge when he comes. For God, who is just is ready to plead Friend's cause, and will give a true judgment. After an appeal to the local county judge, Friends should deliver their appeal to the head of the nation, the king.

Fox understands both the spiritual and the practical aspects of early Friends dilemma. Although he expects Friends to have total allegiance to the Lamb, he still gives detailed instructions about confronting persecutors, preparing documents, and going to court and how to behave there. He has had a great deal of experience of this. He also writes a great many documents confronting trying to change the persecutors minds.

The Lamb's War is an inner war in which Fox patiently accepts suffering and expects Friends to do likewise. However as soon as Friends are beaten, accused, arrested, or have their property confiscated, Fox tells them how to collect the papers that they will need to go to court. He is concerned about day to day life and how Friends are to survive. He is especially concerned about the seizure of property necessary for livelihood. He is not only interested in the spiritual inner life but also interested in Friends as saints living in the world. He is not only interested in life after death but in practical everyday things.

The purity of a Friend's inward life shows us how to live each day. This purity makes us such good persons that we cannot do evil deeds. Fox is saying that we must be such good people on the inside that it spills over in love and generosity to others. This kind of person could not be involved in violence or war.

Early Friends do not fear the devil but arm themselves like men of war, babes and soldiers in the Lamb's war. An inward war fought with inward weapons. spiritual weapons. They stand in the power of the Lamb who supersedes the devil. The only offensive spiritual weapons are the sword of the spirit, the word of God, inspired words. Persuasion, truth, preaching against sin in high places, and confronting persons of high social rank are all spiritual weapons. Fox has confidence in the Word of God, Christ the Word, the written word and the spoken word, all of which were spiritual weapons.

Canby Jones shows real insight – in his book *George Fox's Attitude Toward War* – into the inward dimension of this conflict. Early Quakers refused to take off their hats, bow, or say "you" to individual persons regardless of their social station. Nor, in turn, did they seek deference. In order to be inwardly pure a Friend could not want to be honored by others. When the Lamb had won this inward victory, then the Quaker is ready to witness against the shallow niceties of courtly courtesy. "Hat honor," and insisting on "thee and thou" to all men are relatively minor outgrowths of a total change of the inner life and allegiance of Quakers. (In a P.S. to Letter 53, 1653 Fox writes that to honor all men is to reach that of God in them.)

The conflict of the Lamb's war had other social aspects. Since Christ forbade it, Friends refused to swear oaths. More Friends went to prison for refusing to swear that they are not Roman Catholic agents or for refusing the oath of allegiance to the crown, than for any other cause. After the penal laws of 1661, when Friends held meeting for worship, soldiers barred the doors against them. In the economic sphere, Friends invented the fair price for articles on sale as a testimony against the cheating involved in much common haggling over prices. Fair treatment for the insane, just treatment of Indians and Negroes, also men for whom Christ died, are other aspects of the Lamb's war. Fox confidently expects that the Lamb's war would overthrow social and ecclesiastical evil. Quakers, spiritual revolutionaries, speeded it along.

Religious protesters, Fox strongly believes should not be punished and beaten, knocked down and tumbled up, and struck with cudgels and fists by the orders of magistrates. Although early Friends do not lift up a hand against their persecutors, they are imprisoned as peace breakers. Magistrates should not concern themselves about religion. Fox accuses the state of usurping functions that rightly belong to God. "Where does God have His due," he asks, "when Caesar will have all?

Obligations of magistrates and Friends are clear to Fox. Magistrates set prisoners free and in the future use only spiritual weapons. All the jails should be opened and the prisoners brought out of the nasty holes and dungeons. Friends should not pay taxes to the magistrates, nor worship as they dictate and certainly not bear arms for them. However, they should pray for their welfare. Magistrates are to keep the peace but they are not to bear carnal weapons and fight with the men of peace. Christ is the bond of peace which no man can take away.

Friends have a civic duty to watch for thieves or to spot fires. Persons in positions of secular power and authority, magistrates, could ask this of them. What they could not ask is for Friends to violate their religious principles by forcing them to carry guns. (In some places Friends are fined for not carrying swords and guns.) Fox believes that magistrates have a legitimate right to use force but that they are not to persecute individuals for practicing their religion.

Canby Jones summarizes George Fox's attitude toward war.

1) He believes that wars originate among Christians when they act as traitors to Jesus Christ.

2) He lives in the *Life and Power that Takes Away the Occasion of all wars*.

Fox tries to live that life and power which takes away the occasion of all wars. His job is to be a reconciler, valiant for truth and a fighter in an inward war. This Life and Power is the Lamb, Christ the Royal Seed.

Fox calls men to a spiritual struggle which is "the moral equivalent of war." He calls them to be valiant for God's truth upon the earth, and only fear Him, who can break their fetters, their jails, and their bonds in sunder.

3) Covenant of peace

Fox believes that Friends are called to a covenant of peace to use only spiritual weapons. He relies on spiritual weapons because they are the only ones legitimate for the use of a Christian warrior. The source of these weapons is God to whom all men and women owe obedience:

> our shield is our faith, by which we have victory over all that which separates from God,
> our sword is the word of God
> our baptism is that of the spirit
> our swords are beaten into ploughshares
> don the armor and weapons of the spirit

The purpose of the inward war fought with inward weapons is to bring the truth and blessing of God to men.

4) The Royal Law

The Royal Law, the commandment of Christ, teaches men to love all their enemies, accept suffering as God's gift and bless and pray for those who persecute. One of the important signs that early Friends obey the royal law is their willingness to accept suffering and persecution, loving the oppressor and praying for them.

5.) Christ the King, sovereign ruler of the universe

Christ the King, sovereign ruler of the universe, is the answer to all human ills. He has authority, jurisdiction and power over all men. Everyone owes Him allegiance. *Fox's belief in the universal kingship of Christ is the keystone of his faith and also of his attitude toward war.* Christ begins his rule in the hearts of his saints, and through them He will reign over all the world.

Christ, as King, will judge all nations, send the wicked to eternal torment, bring immediate joy, and deliver the righteous to his kingdom. The Lamb will be victorious.

> *A Benediction: May your meekness and gentleness prevail over the rough and may you be preserved in boldness in the unalterable holy way. The Lord God Almighty preserve you in the pasture of Life, where all the sheep and lambs feed!* Letter 215, 1662

SPIRITUAL WEAPONS

And so, be faithful in his Power you having on the armor of Light, which was before the power of darkness having on the breastplate of Righteousness, the shield of Faith, the helmet of Salvation and the sword of the spirit, which is the Word of God (Eph. 6:14-17), which was before the world was, through which you may savor and discern Wisdom. Letter 252, 1667

Early Friends do not fear the devil but arm themselves like men of war, babes and soldiers in the Lamb's war. An inward war fought with inward weapons. spiritual weapons. They stand in the power of the Lamb who supersedes the devil. The only offensive spiritual weapons are the sword of the spirit, the word of God, inspired words. Persuasion, truth, preaching against sin in high places, and confronting persons of high social rank are all spiritual weapons. Fox has confidence in the Word of God, Christ the Word, the written word and the spoken word, all of which are spiritual weapons. They all have power. Children of the Light and the Day are to mind the Word of the Lord, the word of God within We must grow up in the Living Word Christ who brings the glad tidings of salvation. We will have victory over the world because we know the Word who reconciles us to God. The Light leads us into the virtue of the Word by whom all creatures are made. We have the Word of faith which was in the beginning and makes all clean.

Fox is able to write letters because this is the word of God to Friends.

Fox is also interested in the spoken word. He admonishes Friends not to let our tongues run at random, not to busy ourselves with careless words. For we hear the Light and receive power to bridle our tongues that no idle words be spoken but serviceable ones only. The Light checks us when we speak an evil word for the religion of an individual who does not control his tongue is vain. Every one of us hears the voice which speaks from heaven. The Light condemns and will tell us when we speak evil words.

Fox admonishes us not to be profane and not to make morally offensive speeches. Light tells us not to speak evil of any man. Our conversation should be chaste. Friends who have words – true words, Christ, Scripture – and act contrary to it must go away empty.

Friends don't have to be talking all the time though.

> My dear Friends, be faithful for even though never a word be spoken in your Meetings, you will feel the Seed of God among you all. Letter 77, 1654

If moved of the Lord God, we should speak in fairs or towns. Then as now, preaching on a street corner is a difficult thing to do. Most Friends would be better not to try and do this but instead stay behind in our own Meeting place. Several grown up Friends – strong, mature, devout – should go out to preach the truth. "Grown up Friends" who are spiritually mature. We grow up in Power, in the Living Word, grow in understanding; we grow up as trees of righteousness. We grow up in that which is pure, holy, precious and immortal. We are new creatures growing up in the Light, in the living Word.

In letter 249 Fox writes of the "Word" and "words."

God's Word in your hearts and in your mouth, obey it.
Man is reconciled to God by the word.
Word is near.
Word of God is within.
Word is called a Lamp and a Light.
By this word David is made wiser than his teachers. He saw Christ and called Him Lord.
The Word came to Jacob and he saw Christ and prophesied of Him.
The Word was in the beginning.
Christ's name is "the Word of God."
Word of God is the original language not Greek or Hebrew.

THE KINGDOM OF GOD AND THE SECOND COMING

A Blessing: All honor, glory and thanks be to him forever, who now is come to rule alone in his saints. Rejoice, O all you prophets and righteous ones! The beast, which made war with the lamb and his saints, the Lamb has got the victory over the beast and the ten horns, which pushed at him. Powerful Father and eternal God, to thee alone be all glory, honor and thanks forever. Letter 38, 1653

Kingdom Of God, Kingdom Of Heaven

All Friends, everywhere are to keep out of plots and bustling of war for those who pretend to fight with carnal weapons for Christ are deceived; they fight with spiritual weapons. So his servants do not fight when they are beaten; instead they love their enemies. Friends are called to Christ's peace, not in Adam in the fall. All that pretend to fight for Christ, are deceived; for his kingdom is not of this world, therefore his servants do not fight. His kingdom has both come and is coming to those who give him first place in their lives and loyalties. Christ, the conquering King of judgment becomes Christ the conquering Lamb who will conquer all evil whether individual or universal.

Fox names the Kingdom: Kingdom of God, Kingdom of the Father, Kingdom of Heaven, Kingdom of Christ, Kingdom of His Dear Son, Kingdom of the Lamb, Kingdom of Peace.

We are to seek the glorious Kingdom of God, which stands in Righteousness and Holiness. The Kingdom is present right now so we needn't be concerned about necessities like food, drink and clothes because they will follow. Fox wants Friends to prosper in the world. No less than the Kingdom of God helps us to do this. In primitive times, differences existed among the churches about meats, drinks, days and times but the Apostle said that the Kingdom of God stands not in such things. No one should judge one another about such things for it is below Christians to jangle about them.

The world's people, who are out of the wisdom of God, take thought of what they shall eat and put on; those in the Kingdom of God do not. Saints in the wisdom of God, in the Kingdom of His dear Son, live each day– eating and drinking– all to the praise and Glory of God. For we can do nothing against the Truth and the Truth makes them free.

Quoting Luke 17:21 in letter 300 Fox writes the Kingdom of God is known within. In the Light we inform our minds toward the Kingdom of God which has no end. There we will find love, joy and peace for evermore. We witness this joy in the Holy Ghost.

The Light enables us to see the Kingdom of Heaven. If we go from the Light, it is possible to lose our place in the Kingdom. If we have any kind of addiction, which would master us, it must die or we will not enter into the Kingdom of God. Fox writes in letter 168: No Adulterer nor Fornicator has any part of the Kingdom of God.

The Kingdom of the Father of Life is revealed in Life, Power and Wisdom.

Kingdom Of Christ, Kingdom Of His Dear Son, Kingdom Of The Lamb

The Son and His authority stands over the world, will subdue it and make the kingdom of the world become the Kingdom of the son of God. True peace is known only in Christ's kingdom. We are citizens in this heavenly Kingdom in which all the faithful will be delivered from the power of darkness. All true Christians live in this kingdom in this world and the next.

God translates the Children of the Seed from darkness to Light into the Kingdom of His dear Son. Christ's power in heaven and earth makes the kingdom of the world become the Kingdom of the son of God. Christ the Lamb conquers all evil and bring into existence a new heaven, a new earth and a kingdom of eternal peace among men. Friends are persecuted and suffer. But that's all right because now on earth, among His Saints, the kingdom of heaven has begun; in the future we will live with God.

In letter 245 Fox writes: Here by the law of the Spirit of Life in Christ Jesus you come to know the Lamb's throne, the throne of iniquity thrown down, the chambers of imagery thrown down, and the households of God raised; the fruitless trees thrown down and the plant of God raised up a tree of Righteousness, whose fruit is unto holiness, whose end is everlasting life. So mark the fruits of this tree and the end of this tree.

We need righteousness and holiness to live in the Kingdom now and forever. The "Lamb's throne" is Christ the Lamb, sovereign ruler of the universe. The "throne of iniquity" may be a tyrannical, violent human realm or Satan's realm. Rooms full of idols are "chambers of imagery." A "tree of Righteousness" is Christ.

Kingdom Of Peace

We must seek and enjoy the everlasting Kingdom of Peace in which we come to know peace and the end of war. In the Kingdom of Peace all people live in harmony and neighborliness.
Friends live in the Peaceable Kingdom of Christ Jesus. (The Peaceable Kingdom is the vision of all people living in harmony and neighborliness, seeking the good and welfare of all.) We are to live in and mind the kingdom of Christ the Prince of Peace and not meddle with the powers of the earth. For Friends are heirs of this kingdom. From the foundation of this unrighteous world the Lamb has been slain but has redeemed us. We are not of this unrighteous world but are heirs of an eternal kingdom where no corruptible thing enters. And our weapons are spiritual yet mighty. Through them the strongholds of Satan, the author of wars, fighting, murder, and plots, will be destroyed.

The Kingdom

The Kingdom is "come" and "coming." It is "come;" present within each person who consciously tries to do what God wants them to do with their lives, and who give Christ first place in their lives and loyalties. The Kingdom is also "come" with Christ reigning over the world.

The Kingdom "coming." is the final stage of humanity. The petition:"Thy kingdom come" from the Lord's prayer indicates that Christ thought of the Kingdom in terms of the future. Fox does too. This Kingdom is never to be destroyed. God's goodness becomes the everyday standard for the universe. The Kingdom is not a human kingdom but spiritual and eternal.

An individual who is all light, hasty, airy with a drunken spirit will not live forever in the Kingdom of God. This sort of person is so terrible that he or she should be stopped and judged. All foolishness, unsavoriness and confusion, which causes distraction, the cause of it may be taken away. Light, hasty, airy refers to a state of mind. A drunken spirit is one that is out of control. We have seen this attitude before in letter 56. If we want to spend eternity with God, we should walk worthy of our high calling in God and Christ Jesus, we must be serious and sober with our minds turned inward to worship God, not distracted by the world. T

THE QUAKER PATH OF HOLINESS

Created In the Image of God

So God created man in his own image, in the image of God created he him; male and female created he them. Genesis 1:27

Quoting Genesis 1:26-27 and 5:1 George Fox writes that we are created in God's Image. We can be like God, pure, holy, perfect and righteous. These are moral characteristics. What Fox seems to be saying is that we can be like God, in that we can live good moral lives.

Even though he is quoting Second Corinthians 3:18 in Letter 410: "with open face, behold as in a glass, the Glory of the Lord, and be changed into the same Image, from Glory to Glory, even by the Spirit of the Lord," Fox seems to be describing a particularly vivid and wonderful personal experience.

Of course Fox believes that both men and women are created in the Image of God.

An image is a copy, not the real thing. For we certainly are not God; God is radically different from us. However, we are in God's image in that we know right from wrong, good from evil. We are capable of loving others, of living a peaceful life, of being pure and chaste. If we are to know what it means to be created in God's image, in righteousness and holiness, we have to know something about God, have to spend some time getting to know Him.

Part of being in the image of God is that we can share in the day to day process of creation, have children, teach, write a story, have a garden. We have a responsibility for the environment, are kings and queens over creation and all creatures. God is Love. One way in which we are in the Image of God is that we can love Him in return. We need to love God but we can't love someone we don't know. For real love there must be some reciprocal action. God loves us and we love Him in return. We must try to develop an intimate, immediate, God at hand relationship, without an intermediary.

It is possible for us to lose, or fall from, the image of God if we turn away from His pure spirit. But if we dwell in the Light and wait upon God, He can renew His Image. Then we can be made like God, created anew in His Image, pure, holy, perfect and righteous. Sinners may be healed if they dwell in the Light and wait upon God for He can renew His Image. Christ Jesus restores faithful men and women, as Adam and Eve, into the Image of God and makes them as kings and priests to reign upon the earth. Everyone may be renewed into the Image of God.. For Fox, Christ is the answer; He is sufficient to heal all human ills. For He redeems man and woman up into the image of God, as they were before they fell. In Christ it becomes clear what being in the Image of God means.

What does it mean for us to be created in the Image of God? First it means that we are truly human. It means that we are of value because God lives within us. We can share, in a very small way, with God in Creation. Our decisions are not completely selfish and self-serving but do consider other people's wants and needs. We can live a full life and use the gifts that God has given us.

> A Blessing: May you all work in His Image, in his Power, in his Garden, as man and woman did before the Fall. Letter 344, 1677

All Men and Women Exercise Their Talents

One of Fox's new ideas is that there should be genuine equality for both men and women. He lives in a time when rigid class structure exists with no real equality for men, let alone for women. In our own time – where there is most probably the closest approach to equality for women in the United States that there has ever been – it is not the genuine equality Fox envisioned. He believes that men and women have equal access to God and equal responsibilities and obligations in marriage. Both men and women may use the gifts that God has given them, making the idea of women preachers a reality.

Genuine equality for both men and women has always been a Quaker ideal. But the grubby, everyday reality is that there is very little equality between men and women, between the races. This is why the Quaker idea of equality and value for all people, because God lives within them and has created them in His image, is so important. In a world in which people behave as if created in God's image, there would be genuine equality for all. Everyone would be free to do God's will in their lives; they would be creative and live up to the image of God within them.

In Letter 360 written in 1679 Fox gives a concise, clear statement of the Quaker position on equality of men and women. He also gives the biblical underpinning for this belief.

No Barriers to God

There are no gender barriers to getting to know and love God. "God pours forth his spirit upon all flesh." We are all sons and daughters of God. There may be great ethnic diversity and religious experience but there are no arbitrary intermediaries to cut women off from God, nor men either.

Men are Men; Women are Women

Equality does not mean some sort of unisex to Fox. Men are men; women are women. Men are to be as Abraham, "the father of the faithful," women as Sarah, "a mother of Israel." Women and men, wife and husband, are like Eve and Adam before they fell. Help- meet in righteousness, made in the Image and likeness of God.

Help-meets is an expression used in the King James version of the Bible. A modern translation of the Hebrew phrase might be colleague or co-worker. This is not a relationship of a superior and an inferior being but help-meets, husband and wife, sharing, helping each other. At a beautiful Quaker wedding one of the vows was to be allies, friends working together, not enemies.

Faithful men and women are to be like Aquila and Priscilla, Mr. and Mrs., friends of Paul. They were fellow helpers to the apostles. A congregation, which they began, met in their house, setting a pattern for many Friends to follow.

Faithful Women

When I think about equality, I tend to think of equality for women. The unstated premise is that men have equality so I need only be concerned about equality for women. This is, of course, not so. But Fox seems to be thinking along similar lines when he writes about faithful women and prophetesses such as Dorcas, Huldah and Deborah.

Mary Magdalene, Joanna and Mary, the mother of James, would seem to be first among equals. For it was they who first preached Christ's Resurrection to the apostles. These women were the first to believe and afterwards the apostles came to believe, too. Since God chose women for this special role, Fox seems to be saying, it follows that honorable women may preach and teach.

The apostles encouraged aged, honorable and faithful women to prophesy and be teachers of good things. Aged, honorable and faithful seem a courteous way to describe older women. Fox also writes of excellent old women. He calls women, women and female, does not use degrading labels for them. He also puts up a spirited defense against women being left at home to do the dishes while men are out doing more interesting things.

Both the Old and New Testaments – the Law, Christ and the apostles– support the belief in equal responsibility and opportunity for women. Both encouraged women to prophesy and teach.

Every Man and Woman

Women certainly can have careers. In Fox's opinion the most important of careers – disciples, prophetesses and ministers. Every man and woman is to teach and order their own children.

So that God may be glorified in all their families. Every man and woman should also train their children in the fear of God.

Both men and women have the opportunity to use the talent that God has given them. As husbands or wives, as parents, they both have equal responsibilities. Fox mentions the careers that he knows and thinks are important..

All persons do not have the same abilities. Some have a greater understanding and are better able to teach and stir up others into righteousness. Nonetheless, God makes a way open for everyone and only expects us to live up to the measure within us. For in this measure, which is given to everyone, we may see what is contrary to God. Our job is to improve this measure, so that we can see, hears and understand God's will for our lives. So we are to wait in our measure of the Spirit to learn of Him; keep in the measure of Life and come to feel our strength renewed. Fox emphasizes over and over again that God takes care of us. We just have to stand still in that Power which brings peace.

In Letter 320, 1676 section 5: some women are of a more large capacity and understanding and are able to stir up others into Righteousness in the Power of God. Fox is just complementing these particular women, not saying that women in general are better than men or that these particular women are better than men. Equality – which is for everyone – is access to God, similar responsibilities in marriage and the right to use one's gifts. It is not that everyone has the same abilities.

What Does Equality of Men and Women Mean to Friends?
First and most important is equal access to God. The Lord's people are made up of both men and women. Both men and

women have the same sorts of responsibilities. They also have similar opportunities to use the gifts that God has given them.

In marriage husband and wife are colleagues and co-workers. Again they share similar opportunities and responsibilities.

Because God lives within us as the Light, and we are created in His image. We are members of His family, we are equal. Men and women of every religion, skin color and ethnicity participate in this equality.

PURITY

Mind that which is pure in one another, which joins you together. For nothing will join or make fit, nor unite, nor build but what is pure.
Letter 13, 1652

Fox thought that Friends should lead not just good lives but wonderfully good lives. They should practice the virtues of honesty, justice, purity, modesty and temperance, "live lovely lives of good report." Truth, Purity, Chastity, Faith, Hope and Equality must be part of a good life. Truth is God, the Light, scripture. We should stand in it. To get to know God or to follow our conscious, we must follow Truth and Purity. Chastity is another word for Purity. We should mind the holy life, the chaste life. (Chastity is discussed in the chapter on marriage below.) Faith is that by which we have victory and access to God and the fiery darts of Satan are quenched. In this faith we please God. Hope, the sure anchor, in the great sea the world, is above false belief. It stands keeping the soul up to God a-top of the sea. False hope sinks. (We have already discussed what Fox writes about Equality.)

The basic underlying precept of all of George Fox's beliefs and the one that makes them work is purity. For nothing else works unless there is purity. How is it possible to find the God within ourselves and others, follow our conscience, have faith? We must be pure to know God; we must look to that which is pure in ourselves to lead us to God. We should also look for that which is pure in others and watch over them in love.

Purity is absolutely essential to being a Friend. To our conscience, live a good life, get into heaven, we must be on very close terms with purity. No one is justified living in the "first birth and nature, not in the spirit." We are to live a spiritual life, not a natural one. For nature doesn't purify as God is pure.

We are not to wander in our desires from that which is pure in us. If our thoughts are evil and we have doubts and worries, we are not growing up in that which is pure. If our thoughts are pure, we will know the truth, see things as they really are. **Perfection** may be seen as doing the best that we can. This is a comforting thought but for Fox doing our best is just the starting place.

God is pure; the Light leads us to purity and holiness so that we may be our best selves, our real selves. Christ purifies us as He is pure. We can have a pure heart because pure wisdom is let out of the Treasury into our hearts. Purity is all that is virtuous but it is more than just everyday goodness. It is innocence, untouched by evil and free from guilt. Chaste is a synonym for pure. It means purity in conduct and intention. Holiness is also a synonym for purity. If something is pure, it is not contaminated in any way. Fox uses the term pure in all these senses.

God is Pure, Holy, Perfect, Righteous.

When the word pure is used to refer to God, it means absolute goodness and absolute integrity. We are created in the image of God so we can be made pure like Him. We can be good and act with integrity, be disciplined and capable of holy obedience. This is rather fancy. How does Fox translate integrity into everyday behavior?

> We don't lie; we can be trusted.
> We don't pretend to be something that we're not.
> We follow our conscience.

If Friends wait upon God in that which is pure, they will see themselves as they really are:

> their nakedness (spiritual)
> barrenness
> unfruitfulness
> unworthiness
> hardness of heart

Pure and Undefiled Religion

> Pure Religion and undefiled before God and the Father is this. To visit the fatherless and widows in their affliction, and to keep oneself unspotted from the world.   James 1:27.

Fox seems to like what James has to say and refers to him several times in his letters. Possibly because James has such a Quakerly conscience with his advice on practical love and the avoidance of worldliness. (The King James translates the Greek common gender pronoun in this verse "himself" but with my husband's help, I have substituted "oneself.") George takes the verse and with a wonderful turn of phrase makes it his own. "Pure religion will keep you from the spots of the world." A spotted life is one where there is neither chastity, nor purity. Pure religion is from above, from God, from a source of absolute goodness.

Undefiled religion is free from any contamination. Undefiled can also mean clean. George names God Clean. This may seem an unusual name but Fox uses it as clean as opposed to unclean, something that is filthy or morally impure.

Truth

> Truth is all perfection of Love and Life and Light Letter 142, 1657

Truth is not just the opposite of a lie; it is about real things, not illusions. It is purity, reality, something that is actually experienced or seen. Fox seems to have taken inspiration again from James on how to live a life of purity and truth by helping those in need. He was concerned that apprentices, orphans and all poor widows – those persons who are most vulnerable – should be looked after carefully. Friends should be brought out of the world's feasting and reveling which dishonor the Lord God. Instead Fox advised them to make a feast for the poor, the lame, the maimed and they would be blessed. They are not to invite their rich neighbor or their friends and relatives, anyone who would reward them by inviting them back. Letter 302, 1673 Instead bring the homeless into your homes, cover the naked. Purity and truth are not abstract terms but practical ways Friends should behave.

> Truth makes free from the hypocrite's hope, which perishes and free from Nebuchadnezzar's fury. It makes free from the wild heifer's nature, from the dog, swine, horse, viper, cockatrice and serpent's nature, from the spider and his web, and from oak and cedar, the bramble and briar, bear and lion. The Truth makes free from all these and brings man and

> woman into the image of God. And so, if the Truth makes you free, then are you free indeed. Letter 260, 1668

Friends must always deal with the Truth, be guided by it, be servants to it. Walk, stand up in the Truth. In doing this they will see good and shun evil; hold fast to that which is good and trample all that which is contrary to God. For they know to prize this time while they had it and spend it to the to the honor and glory of God.

The truth is holy, above error and falsehood; the Truth does flourish as the rose among the thorns. None are made free except by it. We should dwell in the truth, keep it and a pure conscious so to triumph in glory. For the Truth leads into a life of modesty, decency and beauty. The devil seeks to destroy the Truth but if we are faithful to it, we will have dominance over him.

Dear Friends, I am glad to hear that the Truth's concerns are so well with you. Letter 412, 1687

Death

> Oh! Be faithful, be faithful to the Lord. Look not back, not too forward. For you have no time but this present time. Therefore, prize your time for your soul's sake. And so grow up in that which is pure, and keep the Oneness, then shall my joy be full. So fare you well! And the Lord God of power keep you in his power! To him be praises forever more! A letter to his mother and father.

This is a beautiful, yet terrible passage. We need only be concerned with today as we can't do anything about the past or the future. It also says that we are going to die. It is reminiscent of the fifth verse of the Thirty-ninth Psalm: ***Lord let me know mine end, and the number of my days, that I may be certified how long I have to live.*** Of course we don't know when we are going to die, which makes doing what is right today all the more important.

We must dwell in purity so that we may understand that which is not pure. For dwelling in purity will guide us to God. We must dwell in purity and wait upon God to receive everlasting Life.   And, of course, Christ is always the answer, the purifier.

A Blessing: The eternal God keep us in his eternal love, pure unto Himself. *Letter 11, 1652*

The Behavior Of A Friend

Keep to the sound language and the honor you have received from above, so that your lives and conversations may preach in virtue, righteousness and holiness, that God may be glorified through you. Owe nothing to any man but Love. So, seek first the Kingdom of God and keep in it. Then all outward things will flow to you, so there will be no want of them. Letter 299, 1673

Fox thought that Friends should lead not just good lives but wonderfully good lives. They should practice the virtues of honesty, justice, purity, modesty and temperance, "live lovely lives of good report." Truth, chastity, faith, hope and equality must be part of a good life. Truth is God, the Light, scripture. We should stand in it. To get to know God or to follow our conscious, we must follow Truth and Purity. Chastity is another word for Purity. We should mind the holy life, the chaste life. (Chastity is discussed in the chapter on marriage below.) Faith is that by which we have victory and access to God and the fiery darts of Satan are quenched. In this faith we please God. Hope, the sure anchor, in the great sea the world, is above false belief. It stands keeping the soul up to God a-top of the sea. False hope sinks. Equality, which means that all people have value, will also be discussed below.

How Should a Friend Behave?

George Fox understands the difference between right and wrong with rare clarity. He had great insight into sin, temptation, and addiction. He makes withstanding temptation sound easy. "When it troubles you," he writes, "just sink down in that which is pure and all will be healed, hushed and fly away."

Good and Evil

Fox uses contrasting words and ideas to point up the difference between good and evil, light and darkness.

Summer, the sun shines and the Light is not dim	*Winter, cold weather and long nights*
Newness of life	*Old life*
Precious, holy, spirit righteousness	*Vile, profane, flesh unrighteousness*
clean, pure	*uncleanness, filth*
abstemiousness	*drunkenness*
careful, wary, considerate, patience	*lying, blasphemy, deceit*
doer	*Sayer only*
generations of the faithful	*generations of the world*
Victory, overcome	*defeat*
Chastity	*Adultery*
Modesty	*Vain, fashion boasting*
Integrity	*Pride*
Spiritual	*Carnal*

It is possible to generate a long list of these opposites showing good and evil. One example will be given in detail. Quoting

John 12:36 Fox writes that Friends are Children of the Light and must turn from darkness. (Children of the Light was the first name that Friends called themselves.) For light is the day, good and shining; darkness is night and evil. Fox also names Friends, Children of Light, Children of the Day, Children of God, sons of God to describe Friends living in the Light. Friends are to wait in the Light to receive the Power to become Children of God. Children of the Seed are of the Kingdom of God for God translates them from darkness to Light into the Kingdom of His dear Son.

Children of the Light, who believe in the Heavenly Light Christ, are not supposed to be just pretty good individuals, they are supposed to be a very good. For the effects of the Light are seen in complete goodness and right living. Children of the Light and the Day live moral lives. They are sober, armed with the breastplate of love and helmet of salvation. They sing and rejoice. Children of God stand in righteousness, put their confidence in God, not man.

Living productive, meaningful lives in this world, loving and serving God is what Fox wants for Friends.

How Should Friends Behave Toward Others?

Friends' first job in behaving toward others is to answer that of God in them and witness to the life of God in themselves. Answer God's witness in all people; answer the just principle of God in all persons. Even captives have the responsibility of answering that of God in others. All persons deserve respect and courtesy. Merchant, professor or farmer should treat their servants and workmen with God's wisdom.

When dealing in commerce—buying and selling—let Truth be the head and practice it. Use accurate weights and measures; don't use fraudulent or deceitful practices; don't cheat. Don't treat your poor customers differently from your rich ones. Quoting Romans 13:8 in Letter 299, Fox admonishes Friends to owe nothing to any man but Love.

Fox understands the temptations that come with money. No matter how much it may seem to be to your advantage Friends are not to
- wrong any man
- covet the possessions of others
- oppress anyone
- live highly on other men's means
- go beyond their capacity
- nor reach after things more than they can justly perform.

Friends are to keep out of debt and keep their word in all their dealings. Any person who has done a wrong to another should be held accountable and ***must*** make restitution speedily.

> But there is the danger of drawing your minds into your business and clogging them with it. So that you can hardly do anything to the service of God, but there will be crying my business, my business. Your minds will go into the things and not over the things, and so therein you do not come into the image of God, in which is dominion. And so, when your minds are got into riches then, if the Lord do cross you and stop you take your goods and customers from you then that mind, that is cumbered, it will fret, being out of the Power of God. Letter 131, 1656

Fox writes to keep out of the bustlings of war; he also writes to keep out of the bustlings of business. Once upon a time a

Friend had a small business and it grew and prospered. It just got too big and too prosperous, so he had to let it go. He, of course, did so but it was with a heavy heart. He had worked hard and had come to like his business very much. But Fox writes in Letter 263 "If we are not faithful in the outward treasure and outward mammon, who will trust us with the true treasure?"

Friends affirm only and cannot swear in court. For taking an oath indicates a double standard. We should always tell the truth. As we have seen in the chapters on the God of Peace, this was important and not an easy thing to do. The admonition to say "Thou" to everyone is the same.

In what may loosely be called social activities Friends must be against:

>   all the false and loose liberties in the flesh
>   all looseness and uncleanness whatsoever
>   all idle tippling, taking tobacco in coffee houses.

Friends are to watch the kind of company they keep and choose sober, serious Friends who love gravity and wisdom. For God has a plan for us and He is the Holy Pattern for this plan.

Sometimes Fox admonishes Friends in pretty standard form. He has stern words for proud boasters who he says are condemned. We should be wise and low and heed knowledge for it can puff us up. Our children are to be trained in the fear of the Lord. We are to live humbly in God's power, prize His mercy; live a righteous, godly life with righteous godly conversation, don't judge. We are to rejoice, love wisdom, be filled with love that thinks no evil.

Then he writes something so insightful. "But above all don't hurt your own soul."

Fox tells Friends, several times, not to be aggravating. The aggravating part of a person is that which exasperates or irritates others. (He obviously is the person who is being irritated.) He also writes them to keep out of Janglings which is grumbling, whining, altercations. A jangler is the person who murmurs and complains.

> If babblers come and janglers say they have a bad meeting, the murmuring nature gets up out of patience. Letter 173, 1659

Fox's moral vision is so clear it must have been hard for him to be patient with others who did not see right and wrong with the clarity that he did. But sometimes it seems impossible to please him. For we should not "let liberty lift us up, nor suffering cast us down."

The world is a dangerous place and Fox knows it. He also knows that God will not abandon His elect, His special chosen people, His Friends. So He gave us our Teacher the Light, to guide us. This Teacher will lead us to purity, holiness, uprightness and open our understanding.

MARRIAGE IN THE MANNER OF FRIENDS

God did move command and join them with his Light, among all the children of Light. This marriage is honorable. Letter 26, 1653

In his book *Uncertain Unions, Marriage in England, 1660-1753*, Lawrence Stone writes that the marriage law as it was practiced n England in the middle of the seventeenth century was a "mess." The root cause of this was that there is no consensus within the society at large about how a legally binding marriage should be carried out. Popular custom, the marriage laws of the church and the state, and the power of owners of property all had to be taken into account.

Village opinion seems to have been satisfied by the outward signs and gestures of marriage, without enquiring too closely into the hard evidence of a legal contract. The church had for centuries enjoyed prime legal control over marriages. A verbal contract, if properly witnessed, satisfied them. However, common law denied that this kind of contract had any effect on the transmission of property. The church also took the position that any ceremony performed between two persons of almost any age, and taking place anywhere and at any time, as long as it was performed by an ordained clergyman, was legally valid.

Property owners objected strongly to secret arrangements and clandestine marriages by which their children could legally marry without their consent. Reform of the marriage laws was hindered because the House of Commons and the House of Lords repeatedly took different sides. The lords favored parental veto over the marriage of minors, while the Commons, which contained many younger sons and small gentry looking for a wife with property, opposed it.

The state was concerned through taxes on marriages and the selling of certificates.

All three branches of the law—ecclesiastical, common and equity—had control over some aspect of marriage. Medieval canon law – revised in 1604—determined the rules of marriage and church courts enforced them. The criminal courts could also become involved if either of the parties chose to sue the other for such statutory penal offences as bigamy or sodomy. These courts interlocked, overlapped, and not infrequently returned contradictory verdicts, about what did or did not constitute a legally valid marriage. There was a great deal of litigation over marriage settlements.

Courtship

George Fox brings order to the chaos that exists in England in the Seventeenth century in regards to marriage laws and recording marriages for Friends. He makes the lines of authority and responsibility clear; he institutes the practice of careful, complete recording of Friend's marriages. He has harsh words against leading someone on and flitting from flower to flower, of men who hunt from woman to woman, or vice versa. These doings are more like Sodom than saints, he writes. One man is not allowed to have more than one woman at once but both men and women may remarry more than once. Bundling, a common courting practice of the world's people in the seventeenth century, is not a practice that Fox would have approved. Instead he writes of the importance of purity and chastity. Chastity before marriage is pure thoughts and abstinence from sex. Chastity in marriage is faithfulness, personal integrity, and responsible sex. Friends should live in the Light which keeps them chaste.

The suitor must ask the parents--her guardian if her parents are dead—of his prospective bride for her hand in marriage. If the parents agree, the couple go to the Women's Meeting first and tell them of their wish to marry. If the members of the Woman's Meeting saw no reason why the couple should not marry, two or three women would go to the Men's Meeting, to tell them of the proposed marriage. Then they could give their judgment and advice to the couple. If a widow wishes to re-marry, part of her late husband's estate is set aside for her children. If either party had been engaged before, they must have a certificate clearing it. If there is any reason for the couple not to be married—if they have some present or past entanglements—it stops here before going to the whole Meeting. If the Men's Meeting finds no objection and the parents or guardian are still agreeable to the marriage, it is allowed to take place. The couple may choose a Meeting, where they please, in some public place, where their family and friends may be present.

Marriage

A man and a woman marry each other. Fox based this on scripture: You are my witnesses this day that I take Ruth to be my wife. Ruth 4:9-11.

Any couple who are married by priest or bishop condemn themselves. For there is no evidence in scripture that it is bishop or priest's work to marry people. It is God's work and His law. The Friends who attend—there should be at least twelve—are the witnesses.

Marriage joins a man and a woman together in the Light. The right joining is the work of the Lord only for it is God's ordinance, not man's. It is heavenly and spiritual, sanctified when the couple follow the Spirit of God. In the beginning God made them male and female. So, in the restoration in the image of God, they are brought to join in one male with one female again. They will live together in Christian marriage, according to God's ordinance and his joining, to be help-meets together as long as they live.

Marriage is honorable, which is why sex in marriage is OK. It is not right to forbid marriage, for this is against Truth and would destroy creation. Everyone should take heed of hurting any concerning marriage. A marriage is forever because divorce is contrary to the Light.

Quaker Certificate

The certificate should be ready, dated, and include the location of the marriage. It should state that such a couple did take one another, in the presence of God, and in the presence of His people. There should be a record of the marriage; there are no secret or clandestine marriages.

The couple being found clear, they are married according to the Law of God and the practice of the holy men recorded in Scripture. They will live together in Christian, honorable marriage, according to God's law and his joining. .

Friends are left "to their freedom" to chose if they want to record their marriage with the magistrate and pay the tax. If

Friends, who did not register their marriage, are cast into prison, then the meeting can produce a document showing that the couple are legally married and send it to the justices so that they can get out of jail.

Christ the Bridegroom

All arise when we hear the heavenly Voice of Christ the Bridegroom, and enter with Him. Enter the wedding feast with Him. Then we are to keep true marriage with Him, the Heavenly Man. our first love, the holy one, the Just one. So all Friends are to speak the Truth and mind that which is pure, the Light of God in them. They are to love Christ and walk in the Light. Then there will be no occasion of stumbling.

(Oil in your lamps refers to the parable in Matthew of the ten virgins, some of whom were prepared with a reserve supply of oil and could celebrate the bridegroom's late arrival.)

> For the voice of the Bridegroom is heard in our Land. Christ is come amongst the prisoners to visit in the prison houses. They have all hope of release, free pardon and to come out freely, for the debt is paid. And he that comes out of prison shall reign .
> Letter 16 1652

This passage, one of the most beautiful in all the letters, shows clearly Fox's belief that all we have to do is stand and wait, Christ is the answer, he does the rest. It has two messages. In encapsulated form it contains all of Christianity; the second is a clear message of hope to Friends who are held in prison.

Remembering Revelation 20, Fox writes "the Seed of the Lamb and his marriage is known." In the Biblical account the lamb's people celebrate; the condemned are not there. Fox has pulled the event forward into his own time. Theologians would call this "realized eschatology" *Eschaton* is Greek for *ultimum* which is Latin for very last. This is a very fancy way of saying that he makes events present here and now.

FRIENDS HAVE POWER

Fox believes that Friends have authority from God to know and feel His incredible Power. He emphasizes over and over again that it is possible to contact this Power. How is this possible? Everyone knows his or her portion and the measure of this living Spirit and Power within. All Friends have two important jobs: to know God and to answer that of God in every person. Getting to know God is Friend's most important job. But it is also important for them to answer the Witness of God in everyone through the authority of the Power of God.

God's Power protects the saints – Fox and Friends – physically and spiritually. While Fox was in prison for eight months, the Lord's Seed and Power protected him; the Power of God expels all that which has darkened the understanding. and which burdens the soul.

A life free from sin is possible because God does not command anything that He does not give the power to accomplish. So there is no reason for Friends to be hasty spirits who run without the Power. For Power keeps down that which would be hasty.

If a Friend was moved of the Lord by his Power to preach the Gospel, they should keep their feet upon the top of the mountains. To be able to do this they should live humbly in God's power and be shod with the gospel of Peace.

> I say be shod all with the Gospel, which is the Power of God, which has brought the Light and immortality to light. I say be shod with the Power, then your feet will not slip nor slide, you will not fall and you will stand steadfast over the workers of iniquity, all unrighteousness in the world and slippery ways.
> Letter 206, 1661 quoting Ephesians 5

Everyone Lives Within the God of Power

Fox believes that God lives within everyone and that it is possible to get in touch with this God within. But he also believes that everyone can get inside the God of Power! For Friends grow up in the Power, skip and leap in, and, as they are saints, have liberty in the Power, partake of It. But the best may be, identifying with Christ the Lamb, living and reigning in the Love, the righteous Life and Power of God doing the Truth to all.

Dwell in the power is a phrase that Fox often uses. Friends should all dwell in Truth everyone according to our measures. All we have to do is stand fast, in that Power which brings peace, stand still in trouble and see the strength of the Lord. We should walk in the Power that is over all, allow It to have supremacy in our lives. Friends should work together, labor together in the Power of God, in His Image, in his Garden as man and woman did before the Fall.

How Friends Should Behave Toward the Power

Friends are not to quench the spirit, nor abuse the Power but be faithful and obedient to it. We are not to add to It, nor take from It, but heed It, pay attention to It. Then we are to stir up others into Righteousness in the Power of God so that everyone may inherit this stable Power. We are to rejoice, delight at the sound of the Power, sing His praises forever, be valiant in the Power of God. But above all we must be careful not to be out the Power of God or lose It.

Following Our Conscience

What guidelines does Fox give on how to follow our conscience? Primarily he gives us the example of his life for he always follows his conscience even if it is the hard thing to do. He is amazingly consistent. We do not lack direction from Fox! The more than 400 pastoral letters tell us how we should behave, how we should follow our conscience. There are no ambiguities, but perfect clarity about what Fox believes.

One way to follow our conscience is to pay attention to the Light in it to lead us to the Truth. Following our conscience means doing what God wants us to do rather than what most people are doing. Following our conscience frequently involves doing something when most other people think that we are wrong and are doing just the opposite. Unfortunately, following our conscience is not necessarily the popular thing to do. We should do what is right no matter how hard the decision or how much it inconveniences us. We should care enough about these things to change our lives.

If we have a genuine concern, we should think it out carefully, go with our experience. We should behave in a decent, honest way, with integrity. When we have accepted a certain way of behaving, we must follow it through, be consistent. If it gets hard, inconvenient, unpleasant, we can't stop even if we make up some elaborate, self-serving explanation to do so. Fox believes that if we listen to God the Light within, not the devil, we will do what is right.

Part of following our conscience is trying to do the will of God Christ also has given to everyone ability according to his measure. Our job is to improve this measure, so that we can see, hears and understand God's will for our lives. God Almighty is among us to do his will in his Love.

The right to conscience must not be trivialized. An opinion, no matter how strongly held, is not conscience.

THE QUAKER PATH OF HOLINESS

> *My dear Friends and brethren everywhere, keep your habitation and your first Love. Do not go forth from your rule of Faith and Life within.* Letter 238, 1664

What is Fox's plan for Friends to follow the Path of Holiness?

First of all, and this really is a rather amazing thing, Fox believes that every individuals is capable of spiritual insights. He doesn't say that Friends are such sinners that there is no hope for them or that they are dammed to Hell for eternity. He believes that Friends are capable of living in the holy order of Life. For they are saints, a Peculiar people, the Elect, the Chosen. For the elect dwell in the Light and do what they profess. 41For without holiness no man shall see the Lord.

Encouraging Friends to live a moral, orderly life, Fox writes that we are to love and worship the Living God who created them in His Image. A deep belief in God is the first step in the path of Quaker Holiness. For God, who made the world, does not dwell in temples made with hands but in us for we are His temple. Friends can't just read about God or rely on someone else's experience; they must get to know God by themselves. It has to be just God and the individual Friend. Friends' job is to turn from darkness and the night, which is evil, to the day and the Light, which is good. So that they may know the things of God.

For Fox everyday is holy; life is sacred. Ordinary everyday activities are sacraments when dedicated to God. All meals, all of life's experiences; all activities have some religious content or intention. Friends were not to keep times and seasons. (They were not to keep the liturgical calendar of the Anglican Church.) No one time is marked out as more holy than another. Every day is Christmas; every day is Easter. For Friends should always remember what God has done for them in the birth and rebirth of His Son.

Quakers are supposed to be everyday ordinary saints, living in the world. No miracles are attributed to them. Quakers don't go up on mountain tops to pray but in the middle of their work places. For God raised up his own seed in his saints. Letter 24, 1652

George Fox was a genius in understanding holiness, moral purity. Friends are to live as pure and holy a life as they can. In Letter 37, 1653 quoting Hebrews 12:14, he writes that we are called into holiness and righteousness without which no one shall see the Lord. (Hebrews says holiness; George adds righteousness.) God wants us to get into heaven but if we don't behave ourselves, we won't. By adding righteousness to the biblical passage Fox emphasizes the moral aspect of it.

We are part of a holy generation and should stand up for holiness. In this holiness we will see God. Of course being George he doesn't let it go at that. For we are to strive and excel one another in holiness, righteousness, godliness, meekness, modesty, in virtue, truth and love. This is not a way of creating unpleasantness in the Meeting for we will forgive others and they will forgive us. We will all live to the praise and glory of God.

To be a holy people, we must walk godly in the holy truth and obey the holy word of God; we must keep holy and righteous to the Glory of God. Righteousness, holiness and purity must wear and outlive all that is contrary to it. We must grow in holiness. For without holiness, we won't see God. We will see God though for He preserves us in his power and the redeemed shall walk in the way of holiness.

Holy is above the profane; Friends are members of a holy generation. For we are to strive and excel in holiness, righteousness, godliness, meekness, modesty, virtue, truth and love. This is not a way of creating unpleasantness for we will also forgive others. To live a holy life we must walk godly in the holy truth and obey the holy word of God; we must keep holy and righteous to the Glory of God. Righteousness, holiness and purity must wear and outlive all that is contrary to it. We must grow in holiness. For the holy way is unalterable, and without holiness, we won't see God. But we will see God because He preserves us in his power and the redeemed shall walk in the way of holiness.

We should know the scriptures and keep in the faith that works by love and purifies us. Our lives must be filled with genuine concern for others and with lots of sharing. It must be simple. To be holy we must follow the path of the just, always looking at the shining Light.

Meeting For Worship

We are the royal priesthood who offers daily to the Lord the spiritual sacrifice, the holy generation and the peculiar people, zealous of good works. George Fox 1659

Friends have an obligation to go to Meeting for Worship which should meet on the First Day of each week. They were to attend Men's and Women's Meetings to do God's business in the world once every two weeks. Meetings should be held even if the number of Friends was small due to imprisonment or for other reasons. Letter 299, 1673 There were no priests similar to Anglican clergy to lead Meeting for Worship. Each Friend was to be part of the Royal Priesthood who offer daily a spiritual sacrifice.

It doesn't make it easier not having a priest, a person to lead the service; it makes it harder. For each person has the responsibilities of the priest. preacher, penitent, confessor, absolver. This is what George Fox means by the royal priesthood and the spiritual sacrifice. Friends are all to be preachers of righteousness, bearing witness to what God has shown us. In the Holy Way they are to know happiness and peace. How do we get to know the things of God? By knowing his son Jesus Christ.

God is Holy Truth. If we mind this Holy Truth, nothing that is unholy will be able to live within us. The Power of God purges everything evil out of our hearts and makes room for Himself.

He will take a broom and sweep out every corner of our house and leave a shining Light

The idea of purity, holiness too, is central to Fox's idea of how Friends should behave toward God and how they should behave toward others. He believes that God demands a very high standard of morality, virtue, goodness and generosity from them.

> Christ says, "Be perfect," and presents men and women perfect to God out of the Fall, up to Adam before he fell, and not only there, but up to himself that never fell, the royal Seed. And so Christ comes to be manifest in people's hearts and the Son to be revealed, who casts out the strong man, which has kept the house and rules in the hearts of Adam and Eve's sons and daughters in disobedience. And so Christ, the second Adam, must rule in people's hearts in the obedience, as he does in all that have Power and enjoy Life. Letter 232, 1663

To sum it all up Friends have to be is perfect . Letter 232 and Matt. 5:48

THE BUSINESS MEETING

An ABC For Grownups About Taking Care Of God's Business In The World

> A Modern Quaker Parable: Once there was a Quaker and at Meeting for Business, he was so obnoxious, so unpleasant, and so manipulative that the Clerk would go home with a splitting headache. Then this Friend became the Clerk. He was empathetic with the members of the Meeting, non-judgmental, loving, selfless, wanting only the best for the Meeting. The best clerk that could be imagined. The moral of this story is that we should all behave as if we had the responsibilities of the Clerk of the Meeting.

A

Accountable
Answerable
Agreement
Attribute

Friends are accountable, answerable, to God, their conscience, and their Meeting.

The object of the Meeting for Business is to reach agreement on how to do God's work in the world.

Acknowledge the gifts of others.

Don't Attribute evil intent to others.

B

Be on time. Be prepared. Be brief. Be open to the Light. Be able to put oneself in the other person's shoes.

The Meeting for Business using consensus is the best way of getting things done with fairness for all.

Begin the Meeting for Business in silence, prayer, humility.

C

Clerk

The Clerk is first among equals. He or she is objective, honest; doesn't hurry the Meeting; gives each person the right to speak. Doesn't allow the Meeting to go on so long that everyone is numb and headachy.
If the Clerk feels strongly about an issue under consideration, he or she may lay down their office to say what's on their mind.

Consensus

Consensus is more than just general agreement, harmony, and accord. It is the way God works through the Meeting.

Courteous

We should treat each other in a courteous manner, have some respect for each other.

If we are courteous to each other we don't shout, interrupt, speak when someone else is speaking.

Comfortable

Be comfortable with differences of opinion.

Community

Quakers don't go off on top of a mountain to practice their religion. They do it in together in community. In a good Meeting there is affection, friendship, members care for each other. A Quaker community should be a joyous and sustaining one.

Conscience

I must follow my conscience. However, I must know what is important and that there is more than one way to serve God. I must do it in my own way and let others follow their conscience in their own way. If I must disagree, it must be done in a courteous way. But I must never confuse conscience with a strongly held opinion.

D

Debate

The Meeting for Business is not a debate. I don't to make points and one side or the other doesn't win.

E

Everyone should prepare for Meeting.
Everyone who wishes to may speak.
Everyone should participate.

Enjoy the Meeting, the members, the celebration of God' love.

Emotion

I may feel passionately, have a great deal of emotion, about certain ideas, beliefs, issues. There is certainly nothing wrong with strong convictions. But, someone else may feel just as strongly in the opposite direction. So at Business Meeting, I must act with discipline and self restraint. State your position objectively. In this way I show respect and courtesy for the other members of the Meeting and don't trample all over them.

F

Faith

Have faith that a suitable solution will eventually evolve.

Have faith and let the corporate spirit work. I might be pleasantly surprised with the unexpected solution that evolves.

When members of a Meeting believe in the same sort of God, are of one mind as to what is the good life, see good and evil in the world in much the same way and agree on what should be done about the evil, it is easier to reach consensus. Where there is not this common faith, the Meeting has to work much harder.

Fluent

The most fluent, the best organized members have a right to speak. So do the least fluent and most disorganized.

Don't Fuss

If there is general agreement, don't go on forever about green or blue carpet.

G

The Meeting for Business is a great treasure.

Good intentions

I should have good intentions, want the Meeting for Business to work. Don't have a private agenda or make a special pleading.

Gang

It is never appropriate to get a gang together and try to win. No matter how serious I may consider the matter under discussion or how misguided I feel the rest of the Meeting is.

Strive not for mastery. Do not exercise lordship over one another. George Fox, 1656

H

Hold each other in the Light.

Don't Hurry. No decision without adequate seasoning!

Hear

For persons in the Meeting who do not hear as well as they once did. One person speak at a time, slowly and clearly.

I

Issue

I don't have to speak to every issue.

Insight

The most far out, difficult person in the Meeting may have the special insight on a problem.

J

Judge

Friends, do not judge one another in Meeting. Your judging one another has emboldened others to quarrel and judge you also. George Fox, 1656

K

Kind

The clerk should be kind, but firm, with Friends who do not behave at Meeting.

L

Listen to others.

Listen to the Light

M

Minute

A Minute should come from the author's experience. It shouldn't ask anyone else to do something that doesn't come out of the way I live my life. I should write the minute from an unselfish point of view.

Member

As a member of Meeting, I should be informed. Speak only from experience. Something that I really know, not something that I read in the newspaper or half remember from a college course twenty years ago.

N

Noble

John Woolman calls men and women the most noble of God's creatures. This certainly is what I should try to be at Meeting for Business.

O

Opposition

Opposition done in a courteous way may help us rethink our own position.

P

Personally

Don't take what other people say personally.

Don't make a personal attack on anyone.

Peace and Patience

Live in Peace, Love and patience one with another.   George Fox, 1669

Q

Quaker Decision Making

There is a good deal of confidence in the way we make decisions. When a Yearly Meeting was unable to resolve a problem, the clerk called for a period of silent worship. Then a Friend suggested a solution that was different from what had been suggested before. It was something that everyone could accept; it was wonderful.

A young Friend lived in an experimental community which made its decisions by consensus. She felt that this day by day experience made her better able to make decisions by consensus at Meeting.

The President of a cantankerous public school PTA board and the chairman of a rather volatile faculty meeting were successful when they used Quaker decision making techniques.

A Friend whose husband was not a Quaker found that decision making on a one to one basis was the most difficult type. When her husband was upset with her, he would say, "Some Quaker!!"

R

Right solution.

Sometimes it would seem that on a particular subject there can be no consensus. However, if I believe in the Light, wait for divine guidance, the right solution will be found.

Responsibility

We have a responsibility to listen and a responsibility to speak.

Revelation

God works through the Meeting for Business. Showing us what He wants us to do, both as a Meeting and as individuals.

S

The Sense of the Meeting is a gift. It comes from the Light to teach us how to make proper decisions.

Query from *Faith and Practice* of Philadelphia Yearly Meeting: "Are your meetings for business held in the spirit of a meeting for worship in which the members seek divine guidance for their actions?"

Stillness, Silence, Lots of silence.

Dear Friends dwell in the stillness and silence of the Power of the Almighty. George Fox, 1661

Stand Aside
I should stand aside if I am not in agreement with a proposed course of action but wish the meeting to move forward. (But read M for minority below.)

T

Twice

Don't speak twice, until everyone has had a chance to speak once.

Truth

Friends should walk in the truth.

U

Unity

Unity means harmony in the Meeting. I should try to find where we have unity.

If I am not at unity with a decision, I must not discuss it outside of the appropriate committee or at Monthly Meeting for Business.

V

Valuable

All persons are valuable because the Light lives within them. So each person has the right to speak and should be listened too.

W

Words

Friends, wait in the Life, which keeps you above words. George Fox, 1656

X

Excellent
Experience

Speak only from prayerful experience.

Y

Yourself
Speak for yourself. Don't ask someone else to do your talking.

Z

Zealous

* * * * * * * * *

Dear Friends, be faithful in the service of God. Mind the Lord's business and be diligent. Letter 257, 1668.

The Clerk should prepare an AGENDA; members should put their concerns in writing. The Recording Clerk should account for all BIRTHS and BURIALS.

The Meeting for Business should

be CENTERED, in touch with God.
be DISCIPLINED.
give EQUAL status to all members.
show the FRUITS of the Holy Spirit.
show us what GOD wants us to do in the world.
not HURRY.

In a Meeting for Business

INTERRUPTING and INTERFERING are not acceptable.
JANGLERS, persons who murmur, complain, whine, or wrangle, can be a problem.
the fire of the Holy Spirit should be KINDLED in our heart.

A Meeting for Business

LAYS down a problem when agreement can't be reached, and comes back to it another day.
allows a MINORITY, even a MINORITY of one, the right to be heard, for they may have the Truth.
NEEDS to be creative and look for a third, fourth, or fifth option.
finds a PEACEABLE, nonviolent, way of handling any problem.
asks Friends to speak QUIETLY. But if someone says, "Speak up, I can't hear you," of course, please do.

REALIZES that of God in everyone.
has a period of SILENCE, when conflict arises. Listens to the STILL, small voice of the SPIRIT.

TESTS our leadings.
uses UNADORNED, plain speech.
has no VICTIMS; everyone speaks their concerns.

is made up of WEIGHTY, seasoned and substantial Friends who understand the business of the Meeting. If this doesn't describe your Meeting, you must pray, work, read, find out all you can   about what it means to be a Friend, until it does.

relies on each person speaking from their own EXPERIENCE.
YIELDS to the power of God so that we can do God's work in the world.
has ZEST for the process of consensus.   Sits back and enjoys seeing new plans emerge.

DAUGHTERS OF LIGHT

Fox calls women in the ministry, daughters, prophets of the Lord. "You are my joy and crown," he writes to them in Letter 35, 1653. Women, as well as men, are to administer spiritual refreshment to all because all are one in Christ Jesus. Fox influences women ministers, as he did all Friends, by the example of his life and his writings. But these ministers also have the example of his preaching, writing and traveling in the ministry. Daughters of Light are orthodox Christians and hold traditional beliefs. They have souls, wante to go to heaven, say "Here am I send me," lead orderly lives of purity and chastity. They leda lives of great bravery and dedication.

Daughters of Light love, serve, and know God. They fear Him but do not quench their prophecy. Holy women must walk in the holy truth and obey the holy word of God, walk in the Light of Christ and grow in His Grace, for the holy way is unalterable. They keep within their own measure, answer that of God in all, wash one another's feet. Fox calls older women mothers in the church of Christ. He defends the right of all women to speak and preach, supporting this with arguments from both the Old and New Testament . Women prophesy and administer spiritual refreshment to all. (See chapter on equality.)

Fox advises these women preachers to speak the Word; neither adding to it with their own reason, nor diminishing from it with a disobedient mind. For the Word is but one. If they have any kind of addiction, which would master them, it must die or they will not enter into the Kingdom of God.

Independent thinkers, Daughters of Light follow their own conscience. They believe deeply in the Quaker faith and are crucial to its spread around the world. Although some lacke much formal schooling, they are smart, capable, successful through their own efforts. They often work alone under difficult conditions.

A meek and quiet spirit, not costly array, is to be their ornament. Fox seems concerned about women following vain fashions in their clothing and writes about his prohibition of this practice in several letters. They mustn't scurry after every new fashion. **Holiness, pureness, and justness must be their jewels.**

Katharine Evans and Sarah Cheevers, two English Daughters of Light, believe that they have a call to travel to Alexandria to preach to the heathen. God wants them to serve Him in this way, use the special gifts that He has poured upon them. He shows His Love, Light, Life in His only begotten son, Jesus Christ.

Sarah wants to obey His "pure call," to preach the everlasting Gospel that would put an end to sin and Satan and bring immortality. Instead they find themselves imprisoned by the Inquisition on the Island of Malta.

Both are married and had husbands and children whom they loved. They write to them from their Inquisition prison in Malta.

    Sarah: My Dear Husband, my love.

Henry Cheevers, my dear Husband

My Dear Husband and dear children

My soul breath to my God for thee and my Children.

Katharine: My right dear and precious Husband with my tender-hearted Children, who are more dear and precious unto me, than the apple of mine eye.

Most Dear and Faithful Husband, Friend and Brother.

My Dear hearts.

While journeying to preach the Gospel of the inner Light, the vessel on which these "daughters of Abraham" sailed makes a short stop at Malta. Katherine and Sarah know that the Inquisition is there and of the possible danger to themselves. In spite of this, they decide to go ashore anyway. They talk to people and distributed books and pamphlets that they have brought with them. (It is possible that George Fox might have stayed on board ship and out of trouble in Malta and gone on to Alexandria to preach. Of course worse trouble might have occurred there.) Sarah and Katherine went on shore in obedience and because they "dared not fly the cross."

The Governor of Malta had a sister who is a nun at a nearby convent. He asks Sarah and Katherine to visit her. At the convent, a priest takes them into the church and wants them to bow to the high altar. This they can not do. So the Inquisitors send for them and asks them for their names and those of their husband and children and parents.   Then they ask:

Wherefore we came into that country?

We were the Servants of the living God, and were moved to come and call them to repentance.

The next day they examined them separately.

Questions for Sarah.

Whether she was a true Catholic?

She answered that she was a true Christian and worshiped God in spirit and truth.

They offered her the Crucifix and wanted her to swear that she would speak the truth.   She answered that she could not swear but that she would speak the truth. They took some of the books that she had with her and wanted her to swear by them but she would not.

Wherefore she brought the books?

We could not speak their language and they might know why we came.
Wherefore she came thither?

To do the will of God.

How the Lord did appear unto her?

By His Spirit.

Whether she did see His Presence and hear His Voice?

She did hear His voice and saw His Presence.

What He said to her?

The Lord told her that she must go over the seas to do His Will.

Two days later the inquisitors came again and question Katherine. They off the Crucifix to her also and she replies much as Sarah had done. They continued with their questions.

Did I own that Christ which died at Jerusalem?

We owned the same Christ, and no other, He is the same yesterday, today and forever.

(Katherine uses the pronoun I and at other times the pronouns we and our. Sometimes in the same sentence to describe their individual and shared experience and belief.)

"Papers from Rome," – from the Pope – and a room (a prison) had been prepared for them. The decision to imprison them has been made before the interrogation. A man with a black Rod, the Chancellor, and the English Consul take them before the Lord Inquisiton who questions them.

Whether we had changed our minds yet?

We should not change from the truth.

What new Light we talked of?

No new Light, but the same the Prophets and apostles bare testimony too.

How came this Light to be lost since then ?

It was not lost, men had it still in them.

Whether we did believe the creed.

We did believe in God, and in Jesus Christ, which was born of the Virgin Mary, and suffered at Jerusalem under Pilate, and arose again from the dead the third day, and ascended to his Father, and shall come to judgment, to judge the quick and the dead.

How we did believe the Resurrection?

We did believe that the just and the unjust should arise, according to the scriptures.

They question them about the difference between Catholic sacraments and Quaker ones. Katherine replies that the flesh and blood of Christ is spiritual and we do feed upon it daily.

Many questions were specifically Roman Catholic.

Do you believe in the Saints and pray to them.

We did believe the communion of saints but we did not pray to them but to God only in the name of Jesus Christ.

While they were in prison, a friar would ask them what day it was. (The name of the Saint's day.)

We did not know, neither did we observe days nor times, months nor years.

(They did not follow the liturgical calendar for Quakers everyday is holy. Because times and seasons are in God's hands. Letter 235 1664)

Whether we did believe in the Catholic Church?

We did believe in the true church of Christ; but the word Catholic we have not read in Scripture.

If we believed a Purgatory?

No, but a heaven and a Hell. (The word purgatory is not in the Bible.)

If we believed their holy sacrament?

We never read the word sacrament in scripture.

The friars tell them that the Pope is the successor of Saint Peter and he could do "what he would." Katherine denies this and says, "We never read any such thing in scripture."

The women's answers that the word does not appear in the Bible might not appear to be a compelling argument today. However in the middle of the seventeenth century the Bible, as interpreted by the Catholic Church, as opposed to Christ's Church, is not only specifically Roman Catholic but Counter Reformation interpretations of Scripture.

The Inquisitors also say that Katherine and Sarah are "fools and asses" because they do not know Latin; their Bibles, books and pamphlets are written in English. It may have been difficult for workers in the field to defend this position. One friar, who often questions them, "fell down of his knees and did howled, and with bitter wishes upon himself if he had not the true faith; but we denied him." The doctor, who is sent to tend to their medical needs, also rages at Sarah because she could not bow to him, but to God only.

When asked which was the true faith, Catholic or Quaker, they answered that everyone had the true Faith that did believe in God, and in Jesus whom He had sent. But those that say they do believe, and do not keep his commandments, are liars, and the truth is not in them. (Obviously a dig at their interrogators.)

The inquisitors had questions about Quaker organization and authority.

Who was the head of Our Church?

    Christ.

What George Fox is.

    A minister of Christ.

Whether he sent us?

    The Lord did move us to come.

Sarah and Katherine are told by the friars that if they will go to mass and receive the sacrament, they might be free. Otherwise the Inquisitors will "use us as they pleased." The Pope will not leave us for "millions of gold" and we shall lose "our souls and our bodies to." Sarah and Katherine reply that the Lord has provided for their souls and bodies which are freely given up to serve Him. He has not committed the charge of their souls to the Pope, nor to the Inquisitors. So a man with a black Rod, and a Keeper, took them and put them into an inner Room in the Inquisition. (The Inquisition is also the name for the building where the offices of the Lord Inquisitor and the prison were located.) The prison room has only two little holes in it for light and air but "the glory of the Lord did shine round about us."

Treatment to Break Their Resolve

Paul was also ship wrecked on Malta.(An account of this adventure may be read in the book of Acts.) The daughters of Light compared their treatment as captives to the treatment that Paul received. The "barbarous" people with whom he dealt treated him well; those who called themselves Christians treated Sarah and Katherine in a terrible way and were not "in the love of God."

The room – their prison – was so hot and close that they would lie down on the floor at the door to try and get a bit of air. They thought that if they didn't have some air, they would die. Several times they mention how hot the room was. They write to the Inquisitor and told him that if he wanted to kill them he could do it some other way as well as to smother them. He took away their writing materials; he had already taken their Bibles claiming that they were false.

Their hair fell out.

Their lives were wretchedly unhappy. When it was night they wished for the day; when it was day they wished that it was night. All they wanted to do was to die. Even so, Katherine writes to her husband, "In our deepest affliction, when I looked for every breath to be the last, I could not wish I had not come over seas."

Right of Conscience

The Inquisition absolutely denied the right to private judgment and the right to one's own conscience. They did not allow individuals to turn to the Light of the Lord Jesus in their conscience to interpret their faith. They also denied the value of the life experience of every individual.

Sarah and Katherine, who believe that they were captives for the Lord's Truth, thought that the Inquisitors were not interested in the Truth but only in trying to entangle them in their talk.

The Terrors of Death Were Strongly upon Me.

The Inquisition wanted to separate them because Katherine was so weak and needed to go into a cooler room. Sarah would stay behind in the hot dark hole. Katherine told the inquisitors that she would rather die in the prison room with Sarah than to be parted from her. They waited five weeks to came back to separate them, but Katherine was ill, broken out from head to toe. The doctor came and said that both would die if they didn't have some air. So their door was opened for six hours a day. Ten weeks later their captors separated them claiming that they corrupted each other. Now Katherine and Sarah would bow to them. However, the more they were persecuted, the more resolute Katherine and Sarah grew.

Various members of the inquisition threatened them with" irons and halters" for preaching the Light so boldly. They threatened that they would be "burnt that night in Malta" with faggots and fire. (But they would not let Katherine have a fire or a candle for more than two hours a day after they separated her and Sarah.) They would be "whipt and quartered." Katherine told them that she wasn't afraid because the Lord was on her side. She also told the friar that "thou art out of the Apostles Doctrine for they were no strikers." The friar tries to defend himself by saying that, in charity, he brought her a doctor

After her torturers leave her, Katherine has a vision and sees the Lord, who tells her that the last enemy to be destroyed is death. This comforts her – the Lord also sends His Holy angels to comfort her – for if she dies under the hand of the Inquisition, she will die innocent and go to heaven. (The Biblical underpinning for this vision is I Corinthians 15.)

No matter how much the Inquisitors threatened, tried to intimidate, offered tempting things, Sarah and Katherine did not relent. They were in a terrible position but not totally hopeless. The first English consul, during their imprisonment, was no help, may even have been an instigator or a collaborator in their imprisonment, but the second consul was more helpful. Like the consuls, the Magistrates were both helpful and harmful. The Magistrates "were kept moderate towards us," Katherine writes. They ordered that their writing supplies should be restored so that they could write to England. Katherine believes that the Magistrate would have set them free if it had not been for the friars. On another occasion though, a Magistrate threatened to take Sarah's bed, trunk and money. She asked him if he were a minister of Christ or a Magistrate. If he were a Magistrate, he might take her money but she would not give it to him.

Even members of the Inquisition said that they were women of virtue, had no malice. The sisters at the convent prayed for them as did the women in the town. When an English ship stopped at Malta, the captain might ask about them and intercede for them, despite the fact that it was at some risk to himself.

Though miserable—hot, tired, dirty, sick, and hungry—they acted with courage, dignity and goodness and used non-aggressive means of defending themselves. They fasted. until Katherine could only lie in bed all day and all night. She sweated until her bed was wet. (What would Fox have to say about women scurrying after vain fashion now?) Smart and articulate Katherine and Sarah know what they believe and can hold their own during the questioning. They also confronted their persecutors. When accused of being heretics, they turned the tables and said that the interrogators were the heretics because they lived in sin and wickedness.

The members of the Inquisition were cruel and terrible men, but also unbelievably petty, mean spirited, and small. One of the friars, an Englishman, seems to always be extremely angry. (This is, of course, one of the seven capitol sins – which are the roots of other sins.) He showed them the crucifix and asks them to look at it, a common ploy. Sarah told him, "Thou shalt not make to thyself the likeness of anything that is in the heaven above or in the earth beneath." The friar went ballistic! He called for irons and chains because—in Katherine's estimation—Sarah spoke so boldly. He blew hot and cold for he turns around and tells them that he would do them any good that he could. On another occasion he tells them that he keeps them away from the Lord Inquisitor to protect them; he is really doing them a service keeping them in prison because the Lord Inquisitor would kill them. It may have also been this English friar who told them that he "would lose one of his fingers" if they would become Catholics.

One of the most amazing encounters with a friar is when one asks Katherine to look at a picture of Mary and the baby Jesus. Maybe she had been asked one time too many to kiss the crucifix or look at some representation of Mary and the Christ Child. "I stampt with my foot and said, Cursed be all Images and Image-makers, and all that fall down to worship them, Christ Jesus is the express Image of his Father's brightness, which is Light and Life." (She and George Fox had the same thought and the same words.)

Power

Katherine calls God Power. (As we have seen earlier Power is the name that Fox calls God most often.) God keeps she and Sarah by His own Power and Holiness. She believes that God would give her power to undergo whatever she had to for His truth. The Lord gave them Power and Words to "stop the mouths of gainsayers of his Truth." Both stand up to their interrogator—calls him a liar and a deceiver—denies him in the Name of the Lord, the living God "for he has no power over me." One of the friars held up his hand often to strike them, but never had the power. He would be quickly "cut down." When a friar accuses her of being possessed, Katherine answers him with one of Fox's most beautiful and hopeful phrases: "the power of an endless life." The hope of a life that will never end, puts their suffering in a different perspective. Katherine and Sarah were kept above all the day to day terribleness of their lives by the "mighty Power of God."

Katherine has a glorious manifestation of God; His Beauty is joy and comfort to her soul. She tells Sarah about this experience, how her Beloved helps her to be less afraid. She has a vision and while "waiting upon the Lord," sees their safe return to England. There she talks to G.F. to her great refreshment. God also refreshes her with his continual Living Presence. By calling God the continual Living Presence, she brings a vividness and urgency to this experience.

When threatened, Katherine believes that the Lord is sufficient to deliver her. She uses a phrase that sounds much like Fox: "a living Fountain." Then she adds a nice twist of her own –"to drink at a broken Cistern." Using Quakerly language she calls Christ, Light and Life, pure Life, the express image of His Father's glory. The Springs of Life refresh the Seed.

Reunited

Katherine believes that the Lord works to bring them together again after so long a time. Five locked doors separated them. The Keeper had not the power to make them fast, for Sarah could undo them. Then they could see one another but could not speak. Their jailers watched them night and day. Yet Sarah came to Katherine's door by night. The jailers discovered her and locked her up again. Apparently they gave their jailers no peace until they opened the doors again. "Then we did sit in the sight of each other to wait upon the Lord so that our voices were heard far."

The Magistrates would hear and bow to it sometimes. Then the complainers were weary and did work to have us brought together and we did wait and pray. The Magistrates would come in often and just look at them and say nothing. So Sarah and Katherine denied them in the Name of the Lord and would declare the truth even if they suffered death. For they could not endure to hear the Name of the Lord blasphemed. Their burdens continued very heavy.

Then one of the friars told them that they had suffered long enough and that they should have their freedom in a few days. An order from the Pope would free them. They could go home on an English ship. Whatever motivated this friar to tell them this, he did not have any authority to do so from his superiors. The Inquisitor came and "lookt down upon us as if he would have eaten us." They did "try us for our lives again and did shut up our doors many weeks." When the Inquisitor came again, Sarah asked him to open the door and let them wash our clothes. So he commanded that the door to be opened once a week. In a little while it was opened every day.

Our Trials Were Unspeakable

Katherine has great affection for Sarah and calls her "faithful friend", "poor lamb" and "my dear and faithful yoke-fellow." The "Enemy" tell Katherine that Sarah will go to Rome and that she will remain in Malta. She wonders why God would leave her behind.

She cries and cries.

Then someone comes and tells her that both she and Sarah are to be sent to Rome. This renews her strength. The inquisitors obviously try to play them off against each other. So Katherine has a vision in which she sees the Pope and the friars standing in ranks and bowing down before her and Sarah!! Even if she and Sarah had to defeat their opponents in a vision, they were never victims.

Katherine and Sarah left England toward the end of 1658. They remained in prison for three and a half years. Between the end of 1661 and the beginning of the following year, the Quaker, Daniel Baker, went to Malta to plead for them. He arranged for the publication of an account of their arrest and imprisonment based on documents and reports they furnished. Finally, they were set free in 1663. Possibly through the intervention of the Jansenist d'Aubigny, the almoner of Queen Henrietta Maria.

A Postscript

Letter 420, To Friends Captive at Macqueness, written toward the end of his life shows many of Fox's distinguishing characteristics. He begins with a tender phrase: with my love to you all in the Lord Jesus Christ. But then continues in a stern manner. Even though the captives are separated from their wives, children, relations and friends, God is with them so they should neither murmur nor complain. Just because they are in a terrible situation doesn't mean that they can behave badly.

He starts with the Old Testament and gives the biblical defense for his position. The captives must be bold and have faith because God delivered Daniel out of the Lion's mouth and He will deliver them also. He continues with the New Testament quoting Hebrews 11: For the righteous were delivered by faith. Then he adds the comfort of Matthew 10:29: For God has all things in His hands and will not let a sparrow fall to the ground without His providence.

Then he lays out their job for Friends while they are captives; it is the same as if they were free. They are to answer the Truth in all, both king and prince. For what do they know. Before the world was made, God may have decided to set them right where they are to preach by their lives and good conversation. Their lives are to shine and they are to be good examples.

Fox believes in the value of all people and that everyone has spiritual insights so every captive may speak to their captors be they kings or princes. He doesn't say that the most learned should speak for the group but that each individual should speak. How is it possible to do this? As always for Fox, Christ is the answer. For through Him the captives have been made more than conquerors. (Letter 414, 1688) They should trust in God's Power and Wisdom and have patience and they will have dominion over all.

Captives should preach in Word, Life and good conversation. In the seventeenth century conversation meant behavior or manner of living. Fox may have been thinking of I Peter 2: 11-12: Dearly beloved, I beseech you as strangers and pilgrims, abstain from fleshly lusts, which war against the soul; Having your conversation honest among the Gentiles; that whereas they speak against you as evildoers, they may by your good works, which they shall behold, glorify God in the day of visitation.

Then he does something that should endear him to many. He adds a postscript. The world is divided between individuals who write postscripts and those who don't. Non-postscript writers have little tolerance for those who do. (Postscript writers often are list makers, too. Fox is and he makes lots of lists.) In the postscript to this letter he advises Friends to petition the most exalted of their captors so that they may have one day a week to meet together for worship and to serve God the Creator. He thinks of details and tells them to write the petition down and have it translated into the language of the person in high position. They should set their hands to this with all speed so that they may attend Meeting for Worship which will give them mutual comfort and refreshment.

Fox continues to the end much as he started. He is both tender and stern with Friends. His knowledge of scripture is great and he depends on the Bible to authenticate his authority. Friends are to live in the Truth.

Good conversation – another way of saying live a good life.

He is clear on how Friends should behave and he holds individuals accountable no matter their condition. Friends should always behave with courage and dignity, preach and be examples.

He loves and worships God the Creator who will protect him with his Power. Since Friends are created in the Image of God, they can speak the truth and be wise.

Christ is the answer to all human ills.

He understands human sin and frailty and does his best to help Friends under persecution.

He works to bring some order to the lives of Friends even those who are captives. They should be a Meeting for Worship, petition the person in the highest position for relief.

He believes in equality for all persons but this brings great responsibility. For each Friend must accept his or her share of the danger connected to this responsibility.

God wishes Friends well; Fox wishes Friends well, too. "I desire that the Lord may grant that you may all be kept and preserved by His holy Power, on His holy Mountain, that you may be the Camp of God."

THE END

Sources

Bobrick, Benson
> *Wide as the Waters the Story of the English Bible and the Revolution it Inspired* Penquin Books, 2002 (WWSEB)

Bromiley, Geoffrey W D Litt
> *Theological Dictionary of the New Testament* Gerhard Friedrich Translator and Editor, Volume V, WM. B. Eerdmanans Publishing Company Grand Rapids, Michigan

Encyclopedia Britannica (BE)

Jones, Canby,
> *The Power of the Lord is Over All*, Friends United Press, Richmond Indiana, 1989 (PLOA)
> *George Fox's Attitude Toward War.* Academic Fellowship, Annapolis, Maryland, 1972 (GFATW)

Quaker Faith & Practice, The Book of Christian discipline of the Yearly Meeting of the Religious Society of Friends (Quakers) in Britain, 1995 Printed by Warwick Printing Company Limited, Warwick (FPYMB)

Stein, Jess, Editor In Chief,
> *Random House Dictionary of the English Language* , Random House, New
> York, 1966 (RHDE)

Stone, Lawrence
> *Uncertain unions Marriages In England, 1660 – 1753*, Oxford University Press, 1992 (UME)

Villani, Stefano
> *A True Account of the Great Tryals and Cruel Suffering Undergone by Those Two Faithful Servants of God Katherine Evans and Sarah Cheevers. La vicenda di due*

quacchere prigioniere dell'inquisizione di Malta. 2003

Walvin, James
> *The Quakers, Money and Morals* 1997 John Murray Publishers Ltd. London (QMM)

Wetherell, David, Editor
> *Dictionary of Friends Terms.* Friends Faith and Life Curriculum. Friends United Press, Richmond, Indiana (DFT)

Endnotes

For a particular word or phrase check the *Sort of Concordance*.

I have used the number of each of Fox's pastoral letter to identify it.

Fox's Testimony, *A Testimony, how the Lord sent G. F. forth at first, in the year 1643,* describes his mission and authority. It is a preface to the 1698 edition of Fox's Epistles. In Canby Jones' edition of the letters, it precedes the first pastoral letter, *Forsake Wild Company*. I have used a T to identify it.

The letter to the Governor of Barbadoes is GOB. This letter can be found in Fox's Journal but I found it on the internet at The Quaker Writings Home Page and copied it from there.

AN ABC TO INTRODUCE QUAKERSTO GROWNUPS DFT	The Fall 2000 Quaker Studies Program, Mountain View Friends Meeting (A xeroxed
1.02.37 FPYMB	copy found in the library of
Chapter 19, Openings FPYMB	Las Cruces Monthly Meeting. No author nor publisher.)
1.02.33 FPYMB	18
1.02.37 FPYMB	70
19.32 FPYMB	38
1.02 FPYMB	4

JRN 1648
RHDEL

INTRODUCTION
252
17
10
64
65
36
244
22
17
249
4
26
286
11
43
18
19
224
30
41
38
75
224
Joy 464, 55,21,52 Let 21, 203, 160, 171, 61

G.F.: NO MAN'S COPY
I am indebted to the reference librarians at the Branigan Library, Las Cruces, New Mexico for finding the quote "no man's copy" on the internet at www.ccel.org. in the *Testimony of William Penn Concerning that Faithful Servant George Fox* which is a forward to George Fox's *Journal*.
17 healed, fly away bustlings, of outward war 232
10
65
36
244
22
17
249
4
26
286
11
43
18
19
224
30
41
38
75
224
Joy 410, 55,21,52 Let 21, 203, 160, 171, 61
Peace, comfort, consolation, assurance, coincidence and satisfaction 206

HOW TO BE A MYSTIC
56

GOD IS ONE

all are subject to One and are one in unity of Spirit. 64
all are one in this faith. 46
children of one father 4
Christ is the Son of God, One in all male and female. 25
Creator 56
Eternal 56
Eternal Spirit is One. 31
Exalted 56
Friends should keep in oneness and unity. 46
God is One. 4, 20, 56
Light   56
Light is but One. 25
Light is One. 4
Living God. 56
Lord 56
Lord God Almighty 56
Lord of hosts   56
One Christ who calls all to repentance 46
One fire which consumes all that the Light discovers to be evil. 46
One Head who calls the repentant up to Himself.   46
One Light who leads you out of darkness into the everlasting Day 46
One Power that raises up the Seed 46
One spirit which baptizes all into one body where there is pureness and oneness.   46
One Eye which is the Light. 46

Peace 56
Light is but one. 64
Power 56
Pure 56
Seed Christ is One 46
Seed   56
Spirit is One 4, 46
Spirit is One.4
Spirit of Christ are One 46
Spirit are One.   44
Wisdom 56
Word is One. 4, 64
Live, dwell, abide in 353

KNOW GOD
Fox writes in his Testimony (T) that it is possible to know God.
to know the things of God for His Truth does flourish.
to know the Spirit of God which He pours on all flesh.
to worship the Living God, maker and creator, Lord of all.
to know his Son, Jesus Christ, who is eternal Life
to know the Power of Christ for He   has all power in heaven and earth.
to know Christ, the second Adam, who enlightens.
to know Christ, the way to God.

to know the scriptures
through the Light

GEORGE FOX'S TIME
Premunire also spelled
praemunire 304, 386
QMM   p. 24
BE
Geneva Bible WWSEB
174-175

GOD OF THE QUAKERS
Also see God of the Quakers
in the supplement.

An ABC of Some of the
Names of God
206
398
  16
   4
235
339
  56
197
164
301
  49
234
  57
235

REFERENCES TO POWER
CAN BE FOUND IN THE
SELECT CONCORANCE

CHRIST   T,15, 19,71, 65,
42 , 52, 56, 6, 16, 355
all Power in heaven and
earth T,189, 355
an offering for the sins of
the whole world GOB
the Light 6
answer 16, 414
answer to all human ills.
420
answer, the purifier. 230
ascended up into heaven
at the end of the world. 33
be comfortable in His death
19
beginning   222, section 8
begins his rule in the hearts
of his saints   9
bore the sins and iniquities
of all mankind GOB
bring immediate joy and
deliver the righteous to his
kingdom 9
bring them to Christ's yoke
65
brings Salvation   305
casts out the strong man
232
comes to be manifest in
people's hearts 232
comes from the Light. 33
comes amongst the
prisoners to visit in the
prison houses 16
Cross   51

170

crucified as he was man GOB
crucified the flesh 44
deliver the righteous to his kingdom 9
destroys the devil 143
died GOB
dwell in the Son of God shall inherit all things 206
end of the Prophets 71
enemies His footstool 206
enlightens everyone who comes into the world T, 42
entered not into the temptation 44
example 64
feeds his sheep and none is able to pluck them out of His hand 355
feel his living Presence 355
fellowship with Him in His sufferings 19
first and last 194, 222 section 8
first love 35
free from evil 16
gave us the Light 29
given to everyone ability 51
glorious gospel 65
God has given to you 306
grow up in the power of His Resurrection. 19
holy one 35

immediate joy 9
in all males and females 56, 320 section 12
in our midst 33
inward (spiritual ministry) 233
joy everlasting 206
judge all nations 9
know T
Life through Him GOB
Life and Power, is unchangeable; earthly things are changeable 76
Light of the world 42
Light justifies you. 62
keep in the Lord's Light 355
keep your meetings gathered into the fold of Christ Jesus 206
Kingdom is everlasting 201
Kingdom of Christ 245
Light justifies you 62
make you free 16
manifest in people's hearts 232
mortifies all evil desires 44
never fell 71
not of this world. 33
our first love 35
paid the debt so that the prisoners have a free pardon. 16

power of His Resurrection. 19
Prince of Peace 300
purifier. 230
restores man and women up into the Image of God. 320, section 12
righteousness 63
rules in the hearts of his saints 9
rules in the hearts of Adam and Eve's sons and daughters 232
Savior of our souls. 33
send the wicked to eternal torment 9
shall reign 16
Substance 71
suffered, so Friends suffer. 30
sufficient if there were no Scripture 320, section 12
tempted but he entered not into the temptation 44
tread on Deceit 19
unchangeable 76
way to God T
yoke 65

CHRIST'S NAMES
Christ T,15, 19,71, 65, 42, 52, 56, 6, 16, 355
Amen 194
Anchor188
Author and finisher 270,(Heb. 12:2)
Baptizer 366
Beginning 222, section 8
Beloved Friend 355
Bishop to oversee you 333
Bishop of the soul 300
Bridegroom 16, 35
Chief Shepherd of your souls 355
Comforter Cross and Crown 414
Counselor to council 274, 311, 333, 399
Day Star arises in your hearts. 270, (2Peter 1:19)
Emmanuel 402
end of the Prophets 71
first and last 194, 222, section 8
first love 35
Governor, who governs his Church in Righteousness 308
Grace 355
Green Tree 344
Head 46, 51, 90, 222, section 8, 399
Heavenly Counselor 313
Heavenly Light Christ 20
Heavenly man 230 265
heavenly Overseer 300
heavenly Priest breaks the peace of all the earthly

priests 300
heavenly Shepherd   300
Heavenly and spiritual man 260, 345
Heavenly Teacher 300
high Priest 355
holy one 35
Holy Pattern 188
Hope of Glory 188
Husband 257,337
Joy 9
Jesus 13, 55, 61, 206, 266
Jesus Christ 355
joy everlasting 206
Light 6, 56 (See entry for Light.)
Light of the world 42
Judge   9
Just one 35
King 9
Leader 306
Life 65
Life and Power 76
Lord 2
one Leader 306
Peace 71
Power of Christ T , 41
Prince of Peace 300
Prophet and Preacher who keeps in His Gospel Order 308
Salvation 65
Savior of our souls. 33
Second Adam T, 71, 232

(See entry for Second Adam.)
Seed 46, 71, 99 (See entry for Seed.)
Son of God 206
Son, Jesus Christ, who is eternal Life T
Son to be revealed 232
Substance 71
Teacher 305, 393
Teacher within 12
Unchangeable   76
Way   T
Word 65

THE LIGHT (OTHER REFERENCES TO THE LIGHT CAN BE FOUND IN THE SELECT CONCORDANCE)

Here are some of the letters that I read to write the ABC and the chapter on the Light. Also see the *THE LIGHT* in the Supplement.

235
100
265
 48
 33
249
 42
 17
266

46
90
53
111
361
27
265
361
244
42
72
71
100

Work in garden
24, 1652
Seed 61
44
Pleasant orchard 183

Creator, the Living God, Life, Father of Life
Creator 292
God of the Quakers 34
Living Light 21

AN ABC FOR GROWNUPS ABOUT WORKING IN THE GARDEN OF GOD
A: 150
B: 48
C: 402
D: 60
E: 235
F: 193
G: 336
H: 336
L: 372, 227
M: 333
N: 95
P: 37
S: 235
T: 65
U; 292
V: 405
W: IS 4:2
X: 371
404
48
402, 76
398
52
339
244
190 and 191
291 and 292
  heavenly husbandman 275
264
dew of heaven 43
God of Truth is a God of Order. 356
245
60,
398
117
60
Blessing 231
40
15
16
384

THE GOD OF PEACE

Peace 133, 134, 155, 183, 217
peace with God 155
God of all Peace keep you. Heb. 13:20-21
Peace comes from the mountain of God. 183
walk in Peace, with the God of Peace, one with another 281
clothe you with the garment of everlasting praise 213
you will have peace and be a blessing to the Lord.   200
promise of Joy, Peace, comfort, and satisfaction 206
peace of God fill your hearts 219
Peace and Wisdom of God fill all your hearts, that nothing may rule in you but Life, which stands in the Lord God. 219
Author of Love and Peace, not strife and confusion. 2 Pe 1:2   244
everlasting Peace 286

An ABC Peace about the God of Peace for Grownups
A: 244, 2 Pe 1:2
B: 353, 1679
C: Heb 13: 20
D: Jas 2:16, 3:18
E: 9, 336
F: 353
G: 208, 158, Re 1:4
H: 300
I: Hag 2:9
J: Rom. 15:13
K: 158
L: 158, 1658; 383
M: 310, 1 TI 1:2
O: 189, Mr 9:50
P: 300
R: 194, 216
S: 383, 232, 401
T: 356
U: 189
W: 219
X: 232, 56
Y: 1 Th 5:13
Z: 55

The Quaker Peace Testimony

The Declaration to Charles II, 1660
 24.04 FPYMB
24.01 FPYMB
300
24.59 FPYMB
24.55 FPYMB
24.06 FPYMB
4
216
215
397, section 6
300

THE LAMB WILL HAVE THE VICTORY
227
 22
249 section 2

239
301
215
227
345
138
143
215
235
Word

GROW UP
grow up in that which is precious and immortal 11
grow up as Trees of Righteousness, which the Lord has Planted 24
grow up in the Light for we are new creatures. 42
grow up in the living Word. 49
grow up in Light 54
grow up in the Power 69

IMAGE OF GOD
32
320 section 12
344
360
390
397 section 1
397 section 2
Second Corinthians 3:18
408
Genesis 1:28
410
39

THE BEHAVIOR OF A FRIEND
EQUALITY
360

PURITY
21
11
79
50
18
31
245
44
6
32
230

MARRIAGE IN THE MANNER OF FRIENDS
ORDERLY AND DISORDERLY MARRIAGES
UME p 131

SOME REFERENCES TO MARRIAGE IN THE PASTORAL LETTERS
abandoning 389
according to God's ordinance 264 section2
acquaint the Men's Meeting L264 1669 section2
adorns herself (Bride)for her husband, Christ Jesus 154
adulterous Eye 154

all may be careful in that thing 389
Apostles told them that marriage was honorable in all, the bed undefiled. 240

ASUNDER
let no man put them asunder 26
bed is not defiled 26, 240, 389

BELIEVERS
marriage of believers and unbelievers   L240

BISHOP
not bishop's nor priest's work to marry 264 section2

break not wedlock with the Lord Jesus Christ 37
bride's clothing   154

BRIDEGROOM
voice of the Bridegroom is heard in our Land.16
true marriage to Christ, the Heavenly Man

CERTIFICATE
carry a copy of the certificate to the magistrate 264 section2
certificate drawn up 264 section2

CHASTE
mind the chaste Life 154

chaste virgin follows the Lamb and goes to the marriage supper of the Lamb154
Light of God keeps you chaste 154
live in that which keeps you chaste (Christ the Lamb) 154

CHILDREN
children were not unholy, but clean. 240
widows, who have children, and intend to re-marry   264 section 2

CHRIST
owns, sets up, encourages marriage 264 section2
marriage in the Covenant and the quickening Spirit. 264 section2
Christian, honorable marriage 264 section2
concerning marriages be careful in that thing 389
command and join them with his Light 26
concerning marriages 26
consent (father and mother) 264 section2
Contract for marriage
make no contract for marriage, break none 389
defile a woman   264 section2
destroy creation 264 section2
do not hurt your marriage 263
do not join together in

marriage contrary to the Light 26
doctrines of the devils 264 section 2
dozen Friends and relations witnesses at a wedding 264 section2
end to all unholiness 37
ENGAGED
engaged, you must have a certificate under the hands of the person, that they have been entangled with 264 section 2
ENTANGLEMENTS
free from all entanglements 264 section 2
have been engaged before must have a certificate 264 section 2
free from all entanglements with any other woman or man. 264 1669 section 2
first love, the holy one, the Just one 37
flirting 389
follow the Lamb of God to his supper and marriage 154
forbid marriage 264 section 2

GOD
God made them male and female. 264 section2
God joins them with His Spirit and Power 264 section2
God's ordinance 389
God did move command and join them with his Light 26
God's ordinance 389
God did move command and join them with his Light 26
grieve their righteous parents.L264 1669 section 2
guardian or trustee 264 1669 section 2
help-meets together 264 section2
holy one 37
janglings there were amongst primitive Christians about marriage 240

JOIN
marriage is a heavenly and spiritual joining 264 section2
joining one male with one female 264 section2
God's joining 389
joined together with the Light are joined together in God 26
joins together by His power 26
right joining in marriage 264 section2
true joining 26
those God joins 264 section2
those who are joined together with the Light are joined together in God 26
whomever God moves, commands and joins together, it was and is by His power 26
joined together with the Light are joined together in God 26

joining is God's ordinance 389
joins together His power 26
judgement and advice to the couple 264 section2
Just one 37
keep marriage with Him 37
laid before the Women's Meeting first 264 section 2
late husband's estate be set out for the children 264 section 2
left to their freedom therein 264 section2
live in the chaste Life 154
live together in Christian, honorable marriage 264 section2

LUST
Lust is against the spiritual fellowship. 154
Keep down the lustful heart and eye for that leads from God and joins with the adulterate in anything. 154
lustful heart and eye 154
lust of the Flesh 154
made promises and then abandoned them 389

MAGISTRATE
magistrate should know it, after the marriage is performed in public 264
carry a copy of the certificate to the magistrate 264
magistrate casts them into prison 264 section2
make no contract for marriage, we break none 389
man defile a woman 264section2
man and a woman marry each other 26

MARRIAGE
marriage is honorable and the bed is not defiled. 26
marriage contrary to the Light 26
marriage supper of the Lamb 154
marriage is honorable 26
marriage is God's ordinance 264 section2
marriage of believers and unbelievers 240
marriage is sanctified. 264 section2
marriage laid before the Women's Meeting first 264 section 2 p
marriage is God's ordinance, not mans 264 section2
marriage is a heavenly and spiritual joining 264 section2

MARRIED
married to the Lord 161
married by priests 264 section2
married to the riches of this world 161

MARRY
marry with unbelievers and

heathen 264 section 2
marry none, it is the Lord's work and we are but witnesses 264 1669 section2
MEN
men who draw out young women's affections L389
men that hunt from woman to woman 264 section2
men leave and go to others 264 section2
MEN'S MEETING
acquainted the Men's Meeting that they have clearness and unity with them and then it may be recorded in a book. 264 section2
two or three women go to the Men's Meeting 264 section 2
judgement and advice to the couple 264 section2
mind the holy Life, the chaste Life 154
more like Sodom than saints 264 section2
no man should speak to a woman concerning marriage before he has spoken to her father and mother 264 section2
not of God's joining, but out of His (God's) covenant 389
one man is not to have many women at once L264 section2
orderly and disorderly marriages 264 section2

out of God's covenant 389
PARENTS
marry with unbelievers and heathen grieve their righteous parents 264 section2
Power of God 37
PRIESTS, BISHOPS
all those married by priests must come to judgment and condemnation 264 section2
it is not bishop's nor priest's work to marry people 264 section2
primitive Christians 240
Revelation 20: the Seed of the Lamb and his marriage is known.
riches of this world 161
RIGHT JOINING
not the work of priests and magistrates 264 1669 section2
the work of the Lord only 264 section2
run from one (woman) to another flirting, flitting and abandoning 389
running hastily together 389
Ruth 4:9: You are my witnesses this day that I take Ruth to be my wife. Quoted in 26
set their hands to a paper and send it to the justices 264 section 2
SODOMY
more like Sodom than saints

264 section2
spirit of God 264 section2
spotted life with no chastity and purity   154
strange flesh 264 section 2
time and place may be set for the marriage 264 section2
true joining   26
unbelievers and heathen 264 section2
Unchaste
unchaste, the Adulterous Eye 154
unchaste follows the whore and the adulterer 154
unchastity will be judged by the Power of the Lord   L154
spotted life where no chastity and purity is 154
undefiled (bed) 240
under age 264 section 2
unspotted life   154
voice of the Bridegroom is heard in our Land 16
widows   264 section 2
WITNESSES
we are but witnesses 264 section2
not less than a dozen 264 section2
witnesses   Ruth 4:9-11 quoted in 264 section2
women whose affections run 264 section2
young women's affections 389
Good and Evil

newness of life 338
profane 38
truthful, praise, reverence, adoration, uprightness 28
doer sayers only 55
defeat   338
proud boasters 34
wise and low 176
train up all your children in the fear of the Lord 5
THE QUAKER PATH OF HOLINESS
 37
254
375
384
196
222 section 9
260 sec.2
215
245

FOLLOWING OUR CONSCIENCE
will of God   401
Christ also has given to everyone ability according to his measure. Our job is to improve this measure, so that we can see, hears and understand God's will for our lives. 51
God Almighty be among you, to do his will in his Love. 197

MEETING FOR BUSINESS

122
116
276
210
119
172, 1659. (Paraphrasing I Peter 2:5.)

An ABC for Grownups about the Meeting for Business
A: 405
B: 48
C: 402
D: 60
E: 235
F: 193
G: 336
H: 336
I: 344
L: 372
M: 333
N: 95
O: 333
P: 372
T: 65
U: 84
V: 84
W: IS 4:2
Y: 275

POSTSCRIPT
other postscripts: 223, 397

Printed in Great Britain
by Amazon